ROBIN FOGARTY ◆ BRIAN PETE

From — STAFF ROOM — *to* — CLASSROOM

A Guide for **Planning** and
Coaching Professional Development

A JOINT PUBLICATION

CORWIN PRESS
A SAGE Publications Company
Thousand Oaks, CA 91320

For information:

 Corwin Press
A Sage Publications Company
2455 Teller Road
Thousand Oaks, California 91320
www.corwinpress.com

Sage Publications Ltd.
1 Oliver's Yard
55 City Road
London EC1Y 1SP
United Kingdom

Sage Publications India Pvt. Ltd.
B-42, Panchsheel Enclave
Post Box 4109
New Delhi 110 017 India

Printed in the United States of America.

Library of Congress Cataloging-in-Publication Data

Fogarty, Robin.
From staff room to classroom: A guide for planning and coaching professional development / Robin Fogarty, Brian Pete.
    p. cm.
Includes bibliographical references and index.
ISBN 978-1-4129-2603-4 (cloth) — ISBN 978-1-4129-2604-1 (pbk.)
    1. Teachers—In-service training—United States. 2. Career development—United States. I. Pete, Brian. II. Title.
LB1731.F54 2007
370.71′5—dc22   2006014224

This book is printed on acid-free paper.

07   08   09   10   11   9   8   7   6   5   4   3   2

Acquisitions Editor:	Jean Ward
Editorial Assistant:	Jordan Barbakow
Production Editor:	Diane S. Foster
Copy Editor:	Robert Holm
Typesetter:	C&M Digitals (P) Ltd
Proofreader:	Dennis W. Webb
Indexer:	Molly Hall
Cover Designer:	Michael Dubowe
Graphic Designer:	Lisa Riley

— *From* —
STAFF ROOM
— *to* —
CLASSROOM

To the adult learner: no longer a neglected species.

Contents

Acknowledgments

The art and science of teaching adults is no easy endeavor!

We treasure the legacy of the researchers and writers who have informed our practice. Accolades to the work of Knowles, Zemke and Zemke, Fullan, Guskey, and Joyce and Showers.

We cherish the professional learning community of learned colleagues who have developed this work with us: Many thanks for the rich experiences with Jim Bellanca, Kay Burke, R. Bruce Williams, Valerie Gregory, Sue Marcus, Carolyn Chapman, Gayle Gregory, Terry Parry, David Kinney, Cathy Sambo, and Elaine and David Brownlow.

We celebrate the true technicians who have worked to make this production possible. We appreciate the talent and toil of Jean Ward, Robert Holm, Connie Collins, Donna Ramirez, Sandra Morris, Dara Lee Howard, and Tim Fogarty.

■ ACKNOWLEDGMENTS FROM THE PUBLISHER

Corwin Press gratefully acknowledges the contributions of the following reviewers:

Catherine Hill
Director of Staff and Organizational Development
Douglas County School District
Castle Rock, CO

Dr. Terri Patterson
Director of Professional Development
Waco Independent School District
Waco, TX

Introduction

This book is comprised of nine chapters that take the reader on a journey with key stops along the way. The first stop offers an introductory look at the concept of change and the theory of how change happens through professional development initiatives. The journey continues with a pause to examine the wants and needs of the adult leaner, "a neglected species" according to early proponents such as Malcolm Knowles. Moving along the path, another highlight is a compendium of best practices in professional development and key elements of effective training models.

Four consecutive points of interest during the reader's travels place the spotlight on the essence of sound practices in working with the adult learner. The narrative guides the reader through the details of effective designing, with the acute understanding that the most critical element in professional development lies in the design format. Subsequently, the reader happens on the golden nuggets of knowledge about presentation skills, the high-profile role of the contemporary staff developer.

With added momentum, the reader glides into the realm of facilitation skills, with additional information on how to become a master at giving up the stage and assuming the elusive role of guide on the side. As the journey proceeds, gingerly, by these crystallized roles of the staff developer, a timely visit to the fourth role, that of mediator or coach, is on the horizon. Working with emerging knowledge and understanding about this most pressing role, the reader gains deeper insights into the skillfulness necessary to genuinely support adult learners in the throes of meaningful, purposeful change.

There are two final yet compelling stops on the journey: the anatomy of a workshop and centers of pedagogy. Joyce and Showers's (1995) research reveals that the most important element of training is the design. This discussion uncovers the anatomy of a workshop, delineating four essential elements of sound training. And, in the last part of this guide, there is a comprehensive discussion about sustaining professional learning through the concept of building communities of learners. Labeled "centers of pedagogy," the discussions thread through the foundational concepts of teacher-to-teacher support, with myriad mentoring and coaching models. The mentoring or coaching segments address various components of the process, including conferencing tools, reflection journals, and techniques for building relationships.

■ A PEEK AT THE CHAPTER HIGHLIGHTS

Each chapter begins with a telling vignette that sets the stage for the targeted input for that chapter. This vignette is followed by a substantive discussion of the topic under examination. The discussions are laced with theoretical underpinnings to the target concept from the key researchers in the various areas. In addition, the practical part is woven into text, as well as set apart from the text, in the form of tools, templates, and tips. Tools include interactive strategies that guarantee a collaborative and active learning component for readers who are putting the ideas into immediate practice. The templates provide the means and measures to engage the adult learners in thoughtful, meaningful, and purposeful ways, as the reader applies the ideas to appropriate professional learning situations. The tips provide dearly held insights into the structures and processes revealed in this guide to professional learning for all who strive to design and deliver powerful professional development.

■ AN INVITATION

Complete in its scope, this edition offers a practical approach to change for those who choose to work with the adult learner in our schools. Peruse the book, selecting a focus of intense interest or ideas that evoke a sense of urgency for your current role, or simply follow the guide from beginning to end, savoring the diversity of elements assembled in this staff development guide for designing, presenting, facilitating, and coaching the adult learner.

Enjoy!

Robin and Brian
Chicago

About the Authors

Robin Fogarty is president of Robin Fogarty and Associates, Ltd., a Chicago-based, minority-owned, educational publishing and consulting company. Her doctorate is in curriculum and human resource development from Loyola University of Chicago. A leading proponent of the thoughtful classroom, she has trained educators throughout the world in curriculum, instruction, and assessment strategies. She has taught at all levels, from kindergarten to college, served as an administrator, and consulted with state departments and ministries of education in the United States, Puerto Rico, Russia, Canada, Australia, New Zealand, Germany, Great Britain, Singapore, Korea, and the Netherlands. She has published articles in *Educational Leadership, Phi Delta Kappan,* and the *Journal of Staff Development.* She is the author of numerous publications, including *Brain-Compatible Classrooms, Ten Things New Teachers Need, Literacy Matters, How to Integrate the Curricula, The Adult Learner, A Look at Transfer, Close the Achievement Gap, Twelve Brain Principles,* and coauthor of *Nine Best Practices That Make the Difference.*

Brian M. Pete, MA, is cofounder of Robin Fogarty & Associates, an educational publishing company, and President of The Education Associates, an international consulting firm. He comes from a family of educators: college professors, school superintendents, teachers, and teachers of teachers. He has a rich background in professional development and has worked in and videotaped classroom teachers and professional experts in schools throughout the United States, Europe, Asia, Australia, and New Zealand. He has an eye for the teachable moment and the words to describe what he sees as skillful teaching. Brian's work on educational videos includes *Best Practices: Classroom Management* and *Best Practices: Active Learning Classrooms.* He is coauthor of five books: *Data-Driven Decisions; Twelve Principles That Make the Difference; Nine Best Practices That Make the Difference; The Adult Learner;* and *A Look at Transfer.*

1

A Guide to the Change Process

Vignette: It's What We Do That Counts

Veteran Teacher: According to Sarason, "Educational change is what teachers do and think—it's as simple and as complex as that."

Novice: What do you mean? Aren't the learning standards evidence that significant curricular change has to occur?

Veteran: Mandates come and go, dictums are sent down, and well-intentioned proclamations are made. Yet, at the end of the day, it's a matter of what the teachers do differently in their classrooms that determines whether or not change actually occurs.

THE CHANGE PROCESS ∎

The Change Process—A Quiet Revolution

The perfect example of the phenomenon described in the vignette is what the authors refer to as the "Quiet Revolution" of the American teacher. This dates back to the 1970s when American educational policymakers declared a commitment to the teaching of the metric system of measurement in the K–12 school environment. Publishers eagerly joined ranks and provided a sampling, although sparse, of metric materials in their textbooks and teaching supplements. And teachers—accountable as always—made no noticeable objections—although they fussed a bit—before they jumped on board and faithfully addressed the pages in their texts. In effect, they did what was asked: They covered the required material, introduced the metric system to their students . . . and, then, continued on with the traditional curriculum, barely taking a breath in between.

Teachers congratulated themselves on a job well done, and rightly so. Not knowing a lot about the metric system, they were not about to embellish the lessons. Yet they had taught the required new material. They felt good about meeting the goal that had been set for them . . . as they eagerly returned to their own ways of measurement.

Oh, yes, they do now revisit those few pages on the metric system each year and then, religiously proceed with what they consider the important parts of the math curriculum. In essence, this is the quiet revolution of the American teacher. There is no outward rebellion about teaching the metric system. . . . Oh, no, it is much more sinister that.

In spite of the fact that liters of Coke and 10K runs have become commonplace, teachers still—quietly and resolutely—reject the entire metric system as an authentic, relevant model of measurement in America. In fact, their quiet revolution has been so effective, metric measurement is still barely taught today in our schools, with the exception of high-level science classes that require the use of metrics.

Change is what teachers do and think. It's as simple and as complex as that.

This, then, is the power of the teacher that the veteran teacher speaks of when he says, "Change is what teachers do and think. It's as simple and as complex as that" (Fullan, 1982, p. 107). Teachers effect change in their domains. That's why the classroom is the site of change, why school improvement occurs—first and foremost—in the classroom, and why the research, unequivocally, supports the theory that teachers make the difference in student achievement.

Now, while this story is told with a bit of tongue in cheek, there are critical kernels of truth that ring true here. Teachers do determine to a great degree what goes on in their classrooms. In fact, it has been rumored that Bruce Joyce, an honored guru in staff development, once said that, "Teaching is the second most private behavior . . ." as he went on to say, "and you know what the first one is."

Yet ironically, this remains the greatest challenge of the staff developer—to convince teachers that they do, indeed, make the difference—in the successes and in the failures—of their students. Even more disturbing for professional leadership is that even if, or when, teachers do see the connection between teaching and learning, some tend to focus on the downside, saying, "We'll be blamed if the kids don't achieve," rather than celebrating the upside, saying, "I am responsible when the kids do well. I teach them in ways that they can learn. I am a teacher in every sense of the word."

Then the question becomes, "How do we as professionals in the field convince teachers that they do make the difference, do indeed determine the degrees of learning success for their students, and do have the talent and tools to ensure the success of every child in their care?" While the research, unequivocally, supports this truth, how do teachers come to believe and embrace the changes that might be needed to accomplish what some of them feel is the "impossible dream"—that every child can and will perform to his highest capabilities?

The Change Game—Myth Versus Reality

To examine the concept of the teaching-learning relationship, it seems appropriate at this point to examine the role of professional development and the process of professional change in attitude, practice, and belief. Guskey (Guskey, 2000) describes the change process within professional learning in this way. From his vast experience in professional learning arenas, Guskey writes about the change that one *expects* to occur in contrast to the actual change process that, paradoxically, *does* occur.

To elaborate the point, there is a story of a young, green staff developer explaining to her supervisor how she thinks this amazing change in teacher practice occurs. She tells how she is going to demonstrate how to teach higher-order thinking skills based on what is known about how the brain learns. Then, as she continues with her hypothesis, "They will be so excited about this emerging research on how teachers can teach to the ways that the brain learns best, that it will change their thinking about how to teach. Armed with this new belief about teaching and learning, they will be eager to go back to their classrooms with new teaching tools, seeing test scores go up and student achievement soar as their students apply more rigorous thinking and reasoning in their work."

Her supervisor, a seasoned staff developer countered, "I understand your theory of change, and I don't want to discourage you or dampen your enthusiasm. Yet that is really not how it happens. Teachers attend the professional learning with a great deal of skepticism. They want to know "it works" before they give up anything they are already doing. So, to change their beliefs, they must be encouraged to go back and try something—to put a new piece into practice. Then, as they see things change with their students, they start to question their long held beliefs and practices. But this process is slow in coming. It requires long-term change models."

Teachers attend the professional learning with a great deal of skepticism.

The freshman staff developer nodded quietly, not really believing what her supervisor had described. She held to her belief that teachers would certainly entertain these new ideas because the research around them was so compelling. New in the field, it would be many years before she thoroughly grasped the complexity of the change process in adult learners.

Yet Guskey documents the very same sequence the supervisor had described. Guskey says that the thinking is often one way, the reality another. As depicted in the chart in Box 1.1, one is the myth, the other the reality.

Guskey's research indicates that when teachers are introduced to ideas and strategies through a professional development experience, they start

---

The Change Process in Schools

Change Process: Is It This?

1. Professional development
2. Change in belief
3. Change in practice
4. Change in achievement

Change Process: Or Is It This?

1. Professional development
2. Change in practice
3. Change in achievement
4. Change in belief

Box 1.1

to think or believe differently only after trying some things in the classroom and seeing positive changes in student achievement with their own eyes. They must see the proof in the pudding that change works before they begin to question what they have always done.

Yet the myth prevails that when teachers learn something new, they get excited about it right away and immediately change their long held beliefs. It just isn't so. As adult learners, they must be convinced with evidence of its worth before they are about to abandon their traditional ways.

Cooperative learning is example. Following Guskey's model, teachers receive professional development in the structures and strategies of cooperative learning groups. They then go back to their classrooms and change their direct instruction practices by adding a cooperative learning task to the lesson. They notice interesting changes in the achievement of some students—kids who had never offered a response now talk in their groups; others take active leadership roles for their assigned responsibility as part of the team; still others show evidence of understanding the information in authentic ways.

> *Yet, the myth prevails that when teachers learn something new, they get excited about it right away.*

As the teachers note these positive signs, they begin to question their long held beliefs that kids learn best through a direct instruction approach. Slowly over time, as these teachers continue to read and learn about cooperative learning, they gradually shift their beliefs. Eventually they institutionalize change by making cooperative learning a critical component of every lesson. But this alteration in belief systems requires many trials and tribulations, as well as much time and energy. Change—real change in one's beliefs—is just not very easy at all.

In fact, even after many years of working with cooperative learning, teachers quietly confess that they still think they should be in front of the class teaching. That's their idea of what teaching is, and it's so hard to alter that view. Although this idea of change through professional development is revisited in the next section, it is important to understand at this point that change occurs first through changing practices, then eventually through changing beliefs. In other words, practices come first and beliefs follow.

Guskey knows that the initial professional development—whether it be in the form of a book study, workshop, conference, or online course—rarely leaves teachers with any change in their thinking about how to go about their craft. Effecting real change takes a sound professional development plan that includes many well-documented elements—from training design to sustained support.

This Horse Is Not Dead

The idea that staff developers and other leaders in the school are in the role of change agents is not new. In fact, Fullan (1982) writes extensively about educational change over time. One overriding premise is that change is not easy. To bring about meaningful change takes time, energy, and patience—all of which must be accompanied by a well-articulated plan that stretches over stages. Adult learners change slowly. They are set in their ways and do not abandon their comfort zones easily.

As educators think about an event or time of change—such as a science textbook adoption, a move from a junior high school to a middle school model, or a shift from the high school bell timetable to a more flexible block schedule—resistant statements abound.

Several tools serve as catalysts for discussion and insight into the idea of the reluctance of adult learners to change. One of the most powerful versions appears as a picture book titled, *If the Horse You're Riding Dies, Then Get Off!* by Grant and Forsten (1999). Box 1.2 shows 12 humorous statements adult learners could easily say when faced with the fear of substantive and meaningful change in front of them. They don't want to believe that the horse is dead.

Listen and you'll hear the creative reluctance that's all too common in the teachers' lounge or in the faculty meeting.

Listen and you'll hear the creative reluctance that's all too common in the teachers' lounge or in the faculty meeting. In examining these comments, there is the definite ring of truth, albeit with a touch of gallows humor.

To demonstrate, the anecdote uses the metaphor of switching horses. The first thing the reluctant learner says is, "This horse is not dead! He's already broken in and has a lot of life left." This reluctance is encoded in teacher-talk as, "I have all my lesson plans done for this!" Others say, "Buy a stronger whip," or, "Change riders." But in education code, this means the staff is not using the horse the right way, and it needs more supervision

We've always done it this way before.

or maybe even new staff members. Still other resistors are heard to lament using the age-old excuse, "We've always done it this way before."

Some are more creative in their resistance and are full of fertile suggestions: "Appoint a committee or a team to study the problem!" or better yet, "Let's visit some other sites and see what they're doing." Others take a more aggressive resistant stance and ask for either an increase in standards or a change in requirements, announcing that, "This horse is not dead!"

This Horse Is Not Dead

1. Buy a stronger whip.

2. Change riders.

3. Say, "This is the way we have always done it."

4. Appoint a committee.

5. Visit other sites.

6. Increase standards to ride a dead horse.

7. Appoint a team.

8. Create a training session.

9. Change requirements, declaring, "This horse is not dead."

10. Hire a consultant.

11. Do a cost analysis.

12. Promote horse to a supervisory position.

Box 1.2

Still others protest that more vigorous action is needed. They put a positive spin on their reluctance to change, urging, "Let's do a cost analysis, hire a consultant, and create a training session to help us." And, finally, the ultimate solution reveals itself when protesters suggest—with a straight face and an earnest tone—"Let's promote the horse to a supervisory position."

These are real comments heard from adult resisters. They are both funny and sad. When put in the context of "This horse is not dead" and "There is no need to change horses," they are hilarious. Yet, when translated as refusals to change to an up-to-date and improved science text, to move to a middle school concept for increased self-esteem and academic achievement of the adolescent, or to schedule by blocks of time in high schools to encourage authentic learning, such excuses ring shallow and false.

The Fear of Change

Here is a story that illustrates the depth of resistance that adults harbor, knowingly or unknowingly, to the change process. Some faculty members recommended an author or expert in the areas of curriculum integration. Subsequently, the staff development consultant was hired by their principal to work with school personnel as they created an interdisciplinary curriculum for students in an alternative degree program. While the principal explained the plan, all the teachers seemed very positive: ready, willing, and able to move in new directions. These same people, however, had been working with the concept of curriculum integration for more than two years, and not one integrated unit had been implemented.

As the consultant began working with the group, the root of the problem started to become all too obvious. The two teachers who, as the cochairs of the committee to integrate curriculum, were supposed to lead the integration effort were, in reality, blocking the team. Each step of the way, at every turn, they would scrutinize the input to the point that all forward progress became immobilized. They questioned, endlessly, the appropriateness of every proposed theme, deliberated about the time frame for teaching the themes, and wondered about the size and makeup of the interdisciplinary structures. Of course, because they were the leaders, others followed their lead.

As the two continually raised thoughtful questions about the various elements of the change effort, others took their objections to heart. Consequently, the group never really made definite decisions about anything. They always left things on the table for further discussion. Well-intentioned as they were, the two leaders were too tentative about actual implementation to move the process forward. Their fear of the unknown prevailed; their ability to accept the ideas, even if imperfect, kept any prospects for change from ever seeing the light of day. Theirs was the power of fear for the adult learner.

Who Moved My Cheese?

Spencer Johnson offers another view of change through his groundbreaking book, *Who Moved My Cheese?* (1998). In this delightful allegory, four memorable characters illustrate how different people approach change with very different attitudes and actions. In Johnson's story, two mice, Sniff and Scurry, and two little human beings, Hem and Haw, each react differently as they discover that a wedge of cheese that has always been in exactly the same place has, suddenly and without explanation, disappeared. Thus, the question each asks himself and others is, naturally, "Who moved my cheese?"

Notice the different paths they take as they deal with the idea of change, as symbolized by the moved cheese. Sniff, the first little mouse, sniffs out the change early and is one of the first to acknowledge its movement and talk about possibilities. Scurry, the second little mouse, scurries immediately into action and starts hunting for the cheese. Then there's Hem, one of the little people, who hems and haws relentlessly about the missing cheese, hangs around, and in the end never totally accepts the reality of his changed circumstances. That leaves Haw, who stays around long enough to embrace the change, even if a bit reluctantly.

Notice the different paths they take as they deal with the idea of change.

Although this story is just an allegory that tells a story about how people react to change, it offers a meaningful platform for further thinking. In fact, readers may want to get their own copy of the book and read the story in its entirety as they track their own reactions to the change process. They may be surprised as they recognize themselves in one of the four imaginary characters.

Go With the Ones Who Are Ready to Go

To illustrate how powerfully accurate this allegory portrays people in the change process, there is a parallel story that actually happened to some real people. It is the story of a small publishing company that was purchased by a large publishing company. As the merger plays out, one employee (Sniff) sniffs out the change early and begins positioning himself for a positive role in the transition. Another employee (Scurry) scurries into action and chooses to leave the company shortly after the merger. A third employee (Hem) hung around, but never really embraces the merger. Hem is on board, yet is not at all happy with the new company. In fact, he complains, resists, and often takes on the role of devil's advocate in company decision-making efforts. A fourth employee (Haw), on the other hand, embraces the inevitable changes and joins the team wholeheartedly. Haw, as it turns out, becomes a valued employee to the merged company as a needed resource, adding insight to decisions through his long history with the company. Each, in very different ways, manages the change.

In the end, the lesson seems to be this: that a change agent must honor each and every reaction to change, as those in the change process are reacting the only way they know how. The change agent must remember that people involved in change are doing the best they can. Some come along quickly and easily, others more slowly, and still others do not come along at all. That is just the way it is.

The best advice for the change agent is, perhaps, to go with the ones who are ready to go. Do not worry too much about the others. And do not let the reluctant ones become a drain on the entire process and zap energy from the project. Allow them to find their own comfort zone and work with them as best you can.

The Tipping Point—Gladwell

In fact, to support the age-old idea of "going with the ones who are ready to go," Gladwell (2000) discusses three excellent theories in his book *The Tipping Point:* (1) the "power of few" to create the momentum for change, (2) the stickiness factor that gives complex ideas the glue for staying power, and (3) the need for a meaningful context with which to frame the innovation with meaning and joy.

In essence, his theory presents the change phenomena as a tiny spark, generated by one or a few, that is sufficiently fueled to suddenly take on a life of its own as it reaches the tipping point. Using another metaphor, this is the kind of benevolent tsunami that change agents yearn for as they try to build momentum for significant change in schools.

The Three-Tier Change Process

Michael Fullan (Fullan & Stiegelbauer, 1991) has been writing about the meaning of educational change for more than 30 years, particularly the concept of change. Fullan's writings offer a comprehensive model for facilitating the change process, particularly in the school setting. A professor at the University of Toronto and charter member of the Ontario Institute for the Study of Education, Fullan offers a simple model for understanding a complex process. He also speaks and writes about what does and does not work as schools and institutions attempt to bring about meaningful change.

One of Fullan's most seminal contributions concerns his three-tier process in Box 1.3 for understanding how change occurs: Stage 1: Initiate the innovation; Stage 2: Implement the innovation; and Stage 3: Institutionalize the innovation.

Three-Tier Change Process by Fullan

Stage 1: Initiate the Change—Introduce the innovation to the participants.

Stage 2: Implement the Change—Apply the tools and techniques of the innovation.

Stage 3: Institutionalize the Change—Establish accountability for continued use.

Box 1.3

Sounds simple enough: initiate, implement, and institutionalize, the three I's. Let's take a more detailed look at each of the three stages.

Stage 1: Initiate

First, to initiate innovation requires planning an introductory awareness that establishes the context, goals, process, and timeline for all who are involved. It means bringing in the big guns or developing a video or powerful multimedia presentation. Initiation especially calls for inclusion of all stakeholders: extending invitations for them to participate, question, acknowledge concerns, and—eventually—announce their level of commitment to the change.

In understanding this earliest stage of change, it is important to note the need to for an energizing level of excitement. Some participants will anticipate the best possible scenario, others the worst. Some are eager to see

Some are eager to see the plan unfold; others dread the effort it will take.

the plan unfold; others dread the effort it will take. Some cannot wait for innovation to begin; others cannot wait until it is over. Yet, for both—the one who anticipates and the other who dreads—the initiation stage signals to all concerned that things are going to change.

Stage 2: Implement

Implementing the innovation takes on another meaning entirely. This is the stage when the plan is put into practice. During implementation, change is applied in real and meaningful ways. Models are introduced through sustained, job-embedded professional development that executes the innovation with integrity and provides the needed input to support the change. It is in this stage that attention is given to the appropriate practice, feedback, and coaching needed to ensure success. In short, this is when the proof is in the pudding. Participants must move past "talk the talk" to "walk the talk" as innovation moves from theory to practice.

Stage 3: Institutionalize

To institutionalize change means that the initial innovation permeates every aspect of the institution, becoming ingrained in its very principles, practices, and policies. Everyone now knows that these innovations have become integral to the overall expectations of all who are involved with the institution—no excuses. This is the way things are done, and everyone is expected to comply.

Of course, to institutionalize an innovation requires persistence and patience. It takes time, rehearsal, repetition, and practice for participants in the innovation to move from novice levels of performance to those of competency and proficiency. It takes financial, emotional, and professional support to adopt an innovation of such magnitude that it is now the essence of the institution. Institutionalizing an idea is usually a long and arduous journey with stops and starts along the way. It is a path characterized by obstacles and challenges, readiness and rewards, faith and fellowship. And when, along the way, levels of achievement are realized, there is some level of satisfaction marked by celebration. These are the celebrations that acknowledge the well-deserved success of the change process and the people who have brought it about.

This brief introduction to the change process is simply the beginning—a testing of the waters. As one might suspect, it is much more complex than described here. In fact, although the process may sometimes sound simple, even Fullan and Stiegelbauer (1991) caution change participants to be aware of the many concerns inherent in the journey. One early concern is that initiating the innovation frequently can take over the entire process. When the initiation process goes overboard, when it becomes too comprehensive, too complicated, and too complex, participants become overwhelmed. They may become worn out in this first stage, a period that can inadvertently go on for weeks, months, and even years. In this case, by the time the implementation stage begins, people may be burned out, negative, and too resistant to do anything more.

When the initiation process goes overboard, when it becomes too comprehensive, too complicated, and too complex, participants become overwhelmed.

This is just one of the many obstacles that interfere with the change process. Be wary. If new to examining and understanding the process of change, the reader may want to take the time to investigate this process more deeply.

Looking at Fullan's Change Process in Action

To illustrate the three phases of the change process as described by Fullan, one would usually look at the change experience within a single school or district. However, sometimes, one part of change for a single innovation works smoothly and is really a fine example for discussion, while other parts may have issues about effectiveness. For this reason in this discussion, each phase is illuminated by the actions at a school or district that presents the change most effectively. The three examples selected are exemplary models of a particular phase of the process of change.

Example: Initiating the Innovation for Change

When a New Mexico school district planned the change from a seventh and eighth grade junior high to a middle school model, administrators decided they would try to incorporate some of the middle school concepts during the change process to ensure as smooth a transition as possible. That decision led to other discussions about what the middle school concept was all about and how to get information about it to various stakeholders. One idea was to hold a town meeting, of sorts, on a Saturday afternoon.

Invitations were sent to about 50 people—board members, principals, teachers, students, parents, and community leaders—to a town meeting facilitated by an expert on the middle school concept. Those who attended then became familiar with the middle school concept, and this beginning step for initiating change had a positive impact on all involved. The initiation plan included follow-up meetings using members of the original group as members of facilitation teams. This plan more than moved the change process off the ground and on its way toward implementation.

Example: Implementing the Innovation for Change

The staff at an Illinois school was not only planning its transition from a traditional bell schedule to a more robust block schedule model but was also in the midst of a building expansion project. As staff members talked about the impact of the block schedule on instructional designs, each department was given opportunities to hear what other departments were doing. The increase in communication across departments was noted by a number of people as a positive, unintended outcome of transitioning to a block schedule.

Ultimately, one of the faculty members suggested that, as they looked at the additional space, perhaps they might want to include a large teacher planning room that would allow members of the various departments to mingle. The rationale was that a common planning space would encourage and facilitate communication across departmental teams. As a result of the suggestion, the staff voted to provide teacher planning space as one large room situated near the teacher workroom where the equipment was housed. Within the large area, a department model for office space was used, with low dividers between the departments allowing easy conversations to take place.

Part of the success of change to a block schedule is attributed to this serendipitous interaction. The planning and teachers' room fostered increased communication among staff, resulting in many integrated curriculum designs and teaming models. The staff not only learned about using the more authentic teaching models recommended for the block schedule but also thrived on the collaborations with knowledgeable colleagues.

Example: Institutionalizing the Innovation for Change

Another Illinois school maintains and supports two professional development building initiatives that have become integral to the valued expectations of both old and new staff members. As part of their new teacher induction and orientation program, professional development offerings are available in the two topics: block scheduling and differentiation. By including specific courses on working with block scheduling and on ways to differentiate teaching, initiatives have become institutionalized and are continuing with their initial and inherent integrity. All are on board and accountable for those processes that are valued in the school's programs.

■ TOOLS TO USE

1. The Change Game

In the change game, Guskey (2000) presents a case for change in schools through professional development. However, the change process he describes may be quite different from the way most people believe change happens. To explore the idea of the change process, readers may want to try a simple exercise. Write the four elements in Box 1.4 on four separate cards or sticky notes.

Elements of the Change Process

- Professional development
- Change in belief
- Change in student achievement
- Change in practice

Box 1.4

Now, move the cards into the appropriate left-to-right sequence to represent how you think change occurs through professional development. If possible, share your thinking with someone else. Next, read what Guskey (2000) says about the complex and elusive process of change.

Note: As discussed previously, Guskey relates that most people believe change within a professional development experience occurs like this: first, participants attend some kind of professional development; next, they change their beliefs about the idea; then, they see changes in student achievement; and finally, they change their practices.

Guskey, however, believes the real sequence is as follows: professional development occurs; teachers change their practices by trying something in their classrooms; they see student achievement increase; and, eventually, they begin to change their belief systems. He claims that teachers change their beliefs only after, not before, seeing evidence of some positive change. Even then, Guskey thinks that change in belief systems occurs over time. It is usually not a sudden "Aha!" moment.

> *It is usually not a sudden "Aha!" moment.*

2. Picture Book

To have a little fun with the idea of how vehemently adults resist change, leaders can use a delightful picture book version of Guskey's statements at a team meeting or a faculty gathering. Look for *If You're Riding a Horse and It Dies, Get Off* by Grant and Forsten (1999) and share in the raucous discussion that ensues.

Quote

As part of a team discussion, team members each respond to the quote, "In professional development, the teacher must use it, not just know about it."

2

A Guide to the Adult Learner

Vignette: Telltale Comments

After working with adults for many years, seasoned consultants find there are some predictable things that adult learners inevitably relate about their professional development experiences. These anecdotes, based on more than cursory comments, are culled from many years of practice with this unique species of learner. However, the following adult learner comments actually reveal the underlying issues and concerns of this group. In fact, each of the quotations mirrors a specific critical attribute of the adult learner's attitudes that reflect in turn on the future fortunes and failures of the adult who teaches other adults.

Telltale 1: *"I hope this isn't gonna be a waste of my time."*
Telltale 2: *"Is this practical?"*
Telltale 3: *"Can I use this right away?"*
Telltale 4: *"How does this fit for my content?"*
Telltale 5: *"Who says this is better?"*
Telltale 6: *"Show me how!"*
Telltale 7: *"I want an expert."*
Telltale 8: *"I don't know why I'm here."*
Telltale 9: *"I'm here with a colleague."*
Telltale 10: *"I already know this!"*

THE ADULT LEARNER ■

In 1995, Zemke and Zemke cited an article that appeared 35 years ago in *Training* magazine titled, *Thirty Things We Know for Sure About Adult Learning.* The title and topic were interesting enough to lead the reader to an even more intriguing piece, a book titled, *The Adult Learner: A Neglected Species* (Knowles, 1973). Grounded within the concept of the adult learner by these two introductions, the authors have gathered together this compendium of current wit and wisdom about this neglected species (Fogarty & Pete, 2004a). Among the entries discussed are ideas about adult learners (Box 2.1) and the roles they play in the adult learning setting.

The Adult Learner

- Who are they? (characteristics)

- Why do they want to learn? (motivations)

- What do they want to learn? (curriculum)

- Where do they want to learn? (time, space, convenience)

- How do they want to learn? (instruction)

Box 2.1

Adult Learning: Nine Findings

Throughout history, the adult learner had gained little attention until 1973 when Malcolm Knowles focused on this population in *The Adult Learner: A Neglected Species.* Knowles drew much needed attention to a group of learners traditionally overlooked in learning literature. His premise, that adult learners are an entity unto themselves, speaks directly to those who teach adults. His belief that there are fundamental facts about the adult learner that are critical to the success of programs that target this particular population has had far-reaching impact in the field of professional learning.

As the prophecy of the information age proclaims, learning is a lifelong journey. Every year, increasing numbers of adults enter formal and informal teaching-learning situations for a variety of reasons. Although adult learners are no longer neglected in the numbers and range of programs available, the literature about adult learners is still somewhat rare. This scarcity of literature is one of the reasons this chapter evolved. It seems timely to publish a current synopsis of the information available about adult learners. What do we know about this growing segment of the learning population? What are the implications for design and implementation? In brief, how might these ideas inform current practices with adult learners?

Examining nine specific considerations sheds light on the early findings of Malcolm Knowles's (1973) writing about adult learners (Box 2.2).

A close discussion of each of Knowles's nine findings offers a more detailed look at the habits and needs of the adult learner. Interestingly, these have been proved true over time and remain respected in the field as this group's prominent issues and concerns.

Knowles: Chart of Nine Findings From
The Adult Learner: A Neglected Species

1. Control of their learning

2. Immediate utility

3. Focus on issues that concern them

4. Test their learning as they go

5. Anticipate how they will use their learning

6. Expect performance improvement

7. Maximize available resources

8. Require collaborative, respectful, mutual, and informal climate

9. Rely on information that is appropriate and developmentally paced

---

Box 2.2

Point 1: Control of their learning. Adult learners want control of their learning. They want to decide what, where, when, and how they will learn whatever it is they have targeted for themselves. Adults want to determine the topic, the location, the timing, and the mode of learning. And each of these decisions is made from an endless range of options.

Adult learners want control of their learning.

Topics: Topics range from high-stakes, work-related skills to personal interests and leisure time pursuits.

Location: The location of the learning extends from convenient and not-so-convenient site locations to virtual learning situations with a personal computer in the home or office.

Time Frame: Learning time ranges from full-time schedules of classes to part-time (nights, weekends, and summer) to anytime schedules of virtual learning.

The Mode: The mode or method of learning for adults is represented by a spectrum of choices that includes face-to-face meetings at actual campuses; field-based cohort group sites; and online, video-based, and Web-based models with chat rooms, bulletin boards, threaded discussions, and office hours.

The choices are plentiful when adult learners are involved. They demand choice, as is obvious from the wealth of learning opportunities that have evolved over the years.

To further illustrate what this "control of learning" looks like, one young teacher raved about the benefits of a video-based master's program in teaching and learning. At the top of her list of pluses was the "anytime or my time" component because she had a new baby. This young female learner admits that if she had been required to travel to a campus site for classes, she would not have been able to earn her master's at that time.

By contrast, one of that same woman's colleagues explained that she could not imagine earning an entire master's degree (10 courses) without substantial face-to-face time with instructors. Both consider the control component critical to their learning choices.

Point 2: Immediate utility. Adult learners are clearly and unequivocally pragmatic. They want to know not just about the utility of what they are learning but also its immediacy. They not only want to use the learning, but to use it now! In essence, adults want to know just how learning interfaces with their needs and how soon that interface will result in meaningful application.

Adults often select learning situations that have a real or imagined sense of urgency. They have decided to take a course or attend a class or engage in some kind of instruction for a reason: They are pursuing an interest, but that interest is in response to perceived needs.

For example, their new learning may be in the form of a new exercise class called "Pilates" or software training in Final Cut Pro (a video-editing program). In both cases, the adult not only seeks out new skills and knowledge but also requires immediate and obvious utility. The Pilates class may be needed to complete a repertoire of appropriate exercise or relaxation options, or the Final Cut Pro may be linked to an impending video project. In either case, the adult learner senses a correspondingly similar level of urgency to learn something new.

Point 3: Focus on issues that concern them. Adult learners are focused learners with specific goals in mind that relate directly to their specific situations. They are quick to question, using particulars that are personally relevant to them. They have almost a tunnel vision focus, looking intently for the connections that are meaningful to their life's circumstances.

> *Adult learners are focused learners with specific goals in mind.*

Adult learners want to keep the spotlight on their own issues and are reluctant to stray off what they perceive to be a most personally relevant track. In fact, adult learners continually and persistently ask extremely focused questions that may concern only themselves. But that is their mission—to learn about the topic and how it relates to them.

A vivid and recurring example illustrates adult learners' need to focus on issues that concern them. When attending conferences or symposiums on the topic of the brain and learning, one or more adult participants invariably relate a personal story to the expert presenter, who is often a medical doctor or researcher in the field. For example, explaining that her mother has been diagnosed with Alzheimer's disease, the participant wants a prescriptive response from the expert. Or another participant goes on about her mother's experience with the neurotransmitter dopamine and requests an appraisal or opinion from the expert about her mother's response to Parkinson's disease.

In both cases, the adult learner makes personal connections to the information and focuses on related issues of concern. These adult learners are constructing meaning through their personally relevant examples, and they expect the expert likewise to connect explicitly with their concerns.

Point 4: Test their learning as they go. Rather than receive background theory and general information, adult learners want to test their learning along the way to mastery. Because they want to know how they are doing as they proceed through the learning experience, adults check the mileage meter intermittently, not merely at the beginning or at the end of the journey. They may want to take little steps but expect feedback on the various phases on their way to final accomplishment. They do not want to get all the way to the end and discover that they have to relearn key elements. They want to keep their eye on the prize and know how they're doing, all at the same time.

Adults check the mileage meter intermittently, not merely at the beginning or at the end of the journey.

Adult learners prefer learning that is specific in nature; they are not particularly interested in overly general or superficial information. Rather, they want a step-by-step process with learning scaffolds and lots of feedback to support their progress along the way. They want the little victories or those mini-successes phase-by-phase, step-by-step, stage-by-stage, part-to-part, and part-to-whole. Skill! Drill!—is their motto.

An example of an adult who is learning about the computer for the first time affirms adult learners' expectations for testing their progress as they go. As a novice, this senior adult enlisted the services of a computer coach to become familiar with the newfangled machine. As the learner progressed during several days of coaching, he insisted on "little performances along the way." From the simple task of turning on the computer to the more complex chore of activating e-mail and searching the Web for medical information, this senior citizen insisted on stopping to demonstrate mastery of each new accomplishment. Although the coach understood the hesitancy of the adult learner to forge forward on the more complex operations, she had not realized the need for testing—and acknowledging—simpler bits of information. The story illustrates the real concerns of adults as learners. They want to know they know, before they get too far along.

Point 5: Anticipate how they will use their learning. Closely related to the Point 2 concerns of "immediate utility," Point 5 recognizes the reality that adults continuously scan their cognition horizons for ways to apply their learning. Often, throughout the entire period they are learning, adults are eagerly anticipating ways to use their new ideas. They look for ways to slot learning into their own personal lives.

Adults have clear and definite expectations for transfer. They are pragmatically poised for relevant and meaningful opportunities to use the new information. In fact, the natural expec-

Adults have clear and definite expectations for transfer.

tation to transfer learning from the classroom to the real world is what separates adult learners from the younger set. Children may learn mostly for the sake of learning, but adults seem programmed to learn for purposeful utility.

One example of such anticipation manifests itself when adults learn a foreign language. If they are taking a Spanish class, it is often related to an upcoming trip to a Spanish-language country. While adults are working hard to learn the language, they are busy anticipating when they will actually be using it. This focused anticipation is evidenced by adults who ask the instructor how to say "vineyard" in Spanish because they are planning to visit the wine country or "bullfight" because that also may be a stop on their itinerary. Although it may sound almost silly to talk about anticipated application—because all learning is for transfer—purposeful utility is a hallmark of adult learning.

Point 6: Expect performance improvement. Parallel to several other concerns mentioned previously, adult learners expect to see their performance improve as a result of their classes or lessons. Adults will sign up for, say, a skiing lesson specifically to develop or hone a particular skill, such as navigating the moguls, and they expect to be better after having taken the lesson.

Of course, adults bring varying levels of skill and expertise to their learning, and they are continually self-appraising as they learn. They expect noticeable improvements and are not shy about saying so. In fact, when adults do not see the progress they are expecting, they are quick to evaluate the instructor as ineffective or unskilled as a teacher. They reason is that they are willing and capable students who have volunteered for the classes. If they are not showing marked improvement, surely the fault must be the instructor's, not theirs—after all, they are motivated learners.

An example similar to the skiing illustration is that of adult learners who sign up for private golf lessons. They are willing participants in an analysis of their grip, stance, and swing—fully expecting to see a notable difference in the execution of their swing. If they don't, adult learners have been known to gripe and complain about the lesson, instructor, equipment, time of day, time of year, weather, lack of weather, and so forth—you get the picture. They expect real improvement, and if they don't see it, they get upset.

Point 7: Maximize available resources. Teachers working with adults have the advantage of being able to tap into the vast experience and resources that adults bring to their learning. The most astute and effective teachers connect to the adult learner's generosity of spirit and wealth of real-world expertise. Mature students eagerly share from their personal vault of tried-and-true resources and experiences, thus enriching the learning process. Their teachers do well by taking advantage of all available resources—photocopies, annotated bibliographies, Web site addresses, and any other available methods—to spur the learning process and make it relevant to the adult learner's needs. A relentless tendency on the part of both teacher and learner to gather and share information and insights creates the richness and depth often found in the adult learning experience.

A perfect example of how to maximize resources for effective adult learning is captured in the graduate education class on data-driven decisions. As soon as the discussion turns to ways to manage the data, participants flood the discussion with the name and description of every kind of data management software known to man. They share a lengthy litany of experiences with various and sundry software programs and hardware companies. By making this information readily available to the adult learners in the class, everyone benefits. Each adult in the room can zero in on the management system that best fits his or her situation. The sharing of resources illuminates the entire discussion and focuses the issues for various adult learners.

Point 8: Require collaborative, respectful, mutual, and informal climate. Adult learners want to collaborate and share. They thrive on the back-and-forth exchange of ideas and the negotiated issues that emerge. Adults are social creatures. They have honed their people skills and are accomplished team members. They understand the power of dialogue and seek advice and input from their colleagues. Adult

Adults are social creatures.

learners know the value of a "reasoned opinion" and have a genuine respect for the thoughts and reactions of their peers. In addition, adults embrace the idea of mutual respect and appreciate the value of mutual learning situations that are somewhat unstructured and informal. They relish the give and take of reciprocally beneficial dialogues and the seesaw of complementary or opposing ideas. Adult learners seek social settings and are stimulated through discussion and expression of ideas.

To exemplify the need for a respectful and social climate of informality and mutual benefits, just think for a moment about a stimulating seminar you may have attended. Think about how exciting it was to have rigorous arguments that exposed different views, sparked further debate, and, eventually, led to deep insight into the issues. This is one example of the collaborative spirit that drives the adult learner.

Point 9: Rely on information that is appropriate and developmentally paced. Adult learners want the learning paced developmentally, without great gaps or giant leaps to remotely connected information or information that goes beyond their comfort zones. They will even say, "I don't want to know about that yet! I just need to concentrate on this part. After I get this conquered, I'll think about the next thing. I can only handle this right now. Don't give me too much, too soon. It doesn't compute."

Adult learners know when they do not know. They are more metacognitive about their learning than young learners. Adults are aware of their own levels of understanding and prefer to move gingerly to the next step. Adults pace themselves and will pace their learning even when the instructor does not honor their need for developmentally appropriate phases. As

> *Adult learners know when they do not know.*

soon as a "leap" is sensed, they back up and almost demand a more logical and incremental path.

An example that comes to mind is of two couples learning to play bridge. One of the four is an expert bridge player and has taken on the task of teaching the other three. The three adults learning about bridge come to the table with various levels of understanding and actual experience with the game itself. As the instruction progresses, the expert tries to move from the fundamentals of arranging the hand and counting points to the concept of a game, a partial game, and a rubber. As soon as he starts to describe the elements of scoring, all three adult learners protest. They are focused on counting their points and trying to determine appropriate bids based on their hands. They are not able to shift focus and consider the bid in reference to winning a game or rubber. They simply are not there yet. Developmentally, they are not ready to tackle anything else. They want to succeed at this bidding stage first.

Five Assumptions About the Adult Learner

In *The Adult Learner: A Neglected Species* (1973), Malcolm Knowles presents a comprehensive adult learning theory. He uses the term "androgogy," coined by Kapp in 1833 and developed by Lindeman in 1926 to describe "the art and science of helping adults learn." For Knowles, androgogy takes on a broader meaning, one that refers to learner-focused education for all ages. Knowles believes that androgogy is process oriented rather than content based (pedagogy). He anchors his theory on five main assumptions as depicted in Box 2.3.

Five Assumptions About Adult Learners

1. Self-concept: The adult learner moves toward a self-directed human being.
2. Experience: The adult learner accumulates a personal growing reservoir of experiences.
3. Readiness to learn: The adult learner is oriented to developmental tasks of social roles.
4. Orientation to learning: The adult learner is problem centered and aware of the immediacy of application.
5. Motivation: The adult learner harbors internal motivation.

Box 2.3

Self-concept of the adult learners. The evolving self-concept of adult learners is one that is moving from a dependent personality toward that of a self-directed human being. Adult learners are directing their own plan. They schedule learning into busy calendars, and they do their own diagnosing and prescribing about what learning opportunities they need and what they will embrace. Adult learners are, in effect, driven by their individual concepts of self.

Experience of the adult learners. As people mature, they are constantly and continually adding to their expanding reservoir of experiences. This phenomenon of an ever deepening well of knowledge provides an increasing resource for learning. Adult learners bring much to the table. The traditional concept of "tabula rasa," or blank slate, in no way applies to the adult learner. Rather, adult learners have a rich and extensive bank of experiences from which to draw.

Adult learners' readiness to learn. Adults' eagerness to learn is anchored to developmental tasks that are necessary for their social roles, whether at home, work, or in the community. In other words, adults are focused and ready in a highly pragmatic way. They are eager to learn skills, concepts, and attitudes that are obviously and directly related to their work, families, or themselves. They want to learn those things that will make their lives easier or better in some substantive way. In fact, they are so focused on application that the phrase, "Ready! Fire! Aim!" sometimes applies.

Ready! Fire! Aim!

Adult learners' orientation to learn. As suggested previously, adult learners approach learning with a sense of urgency. They want an immediacy of application and are poised to use the new learning in real problem-centered ways. In fact, they expect to apply their learning at once, to fulfill a need or address an issue. Again, adult learners are highly oriented to learning for an immediate purpose or impending concern.

Adult learners' motivation to learn. Adult learners have an intrinsic motivation to learn. They are self-directed, eager learners, or "omnivores," who devour everything and anything connected to their goals. They can't get enough, fast enough, to make them happy. Adult learners are learning for a reason, and they push themselves from within. They are sparked by an inner source that fuels their sense of urgency to learn.

Although Knowles's 1973 work is still considered the most important of its kind, his classic book on adult learners has been revised and updated as *The Adult Learner: The Definitive Classic in Adult Education and Human Resource Development* (Knowles, Holton, & Swanson, 1998). While preserving the best of Knowles's previous edition, Holton and Swanson also incorporated the latest developments in adult learning theory and practice.

Supporting Assumptions About Adult Learners

Complementary studies reveal a list of assumptions similar to those of Knowles that support his findings. He cites Dirk, Lavin, and Pelavin, who in 1995 stated that experts generally agree on the four assumptions listed in Box 2.4. Readers will note how these four assumptions are subsumed within Knowles's original nine.

Four Supporting Assumptions About Adult Learners

1. Diverse, active learners

2. Problem oriented

3. Control their own learning

4. Strong sense of self

Box 2.4

Diverse, active learners. Adult learners are diverse learners, bringing a wealth of life experiences to their learning activity. Although they vary widely in age, abilities, level of schooling, job experiences, cultural background, and personal goals, they all carry a reservoir of personal experiences that serve them well in new learning situations.

Adult learners are problem oriented. Adult learners want to relate their learning to specific contexts in their lives, ones that usually involve work, their homes and families, or their avocations. While they tend to be pragmatic learners and seek to improve their performance, schoolwork takes a back seat to other responsibilities. Because they are busy people with many items on their plates, adult learners expect their class time to be well spent and anticipate that their course will help them address existing problems.

> *Adult learners want to relate their learning to specific contexts in their lives.*

Control over their own learning. Adult learners tend to be voluntary learners who take seriously their decision to return to school. They believe that education will be helpful and want to exercise some degree of control over their learning. Their maturity level and familiarity with content often determines a greater or lesser degree of self-directedness.

Strong sense of self. Adult learners, naturally, have varying degrees of self-efficacy; but for the most part, they demonstrate a strong sense of self in their learning. Even so, some feel embarrassed about returning to school or joining classes of younger students. Some may hold negative

---
Adult learners, naturally, have varying degrees of self-efficacy.

---

impressions of their own abilities or schools, teachers, and educational experiences in general. They may have varying levels of awareness about their own learning styles. Still, adult learners' sense of self greatly enhances the meaningfulness of their learning, the effectiveness of the learning situation, and their sense of accomplishment.

Thirty Things We Know for Sure

Zemke and Zemke (1995) present a comprehensive summary of some things we know for sure about the adult learner in their classic article by the same name that appeared in the 1990s. A glance at the article, *Thirty Things We Know for Sure*, reveals three categorical areas in which the authors present a cogent view of the adult learner. These categories include motivation to learn, curriculum design, and classroom instructional designs. Below is a brief, more detailed discussion of the article.

Motivation to Learn

1. Preference for real-world, problem-based approaches

2. Opportunity for personal growth or gain

3. The role of increased participation in motivating the adult learner

Curricular Designs

1. Problem-centered curriculum models

2. The need for preassessments

3. Integration of information

4. Fidelity in case studies and exercises

5. Feedback and recognition

6. Accommodation of various learning styles

7. Accommodation of adults' continued growth and changing values

8. The need for transfer strategies

In the Classroom

1. The ideas of a safe learning environment

2. The preference for facilitation rather than lecture mode

3. Methods and techniques for promoting understanding and fostering transfer

Implications

What does all this mean for the site-based staff developer? In considering how to maximize the adult learning experience, there are important implications for the site-based staff developer who understands what is known about the adult learner. The implications range from questions about how to design adult learning to its relevant application in the workplace.

> *What does all this mean for the site-based staff developer?*

More specifically, staff developers need to consider how best to work directly and indirectly with adult learners, what roles adult learners play in learning settings, how best to facilitate change with adults, and how to maintain and sustain the learning once adult learners are on their own.

Following the introductory chapters on change theory, adult learners, and professional development, there are four major chapters that address the roles of design, presentation, facilitation, and coaching. Chapter 4 presents forms and formats that create effective training designs and productive workshop models. Chapter 5 continues with the essential skills of memorable presentations. Chapter 6, in turn, focuses on facilitation strategies for collaborative learning, while Chapter 7 emphasizes the absolutely critical component of coaching for transfer and application. The book ends by looking at the research-based elements of the training model and ways of sustaining and maintaining professional development's positive effects through the establishment of learning communities called "centers of pedagogy." There's one aspect of the adult learner to explore before going forward, however. It concerns the informal roles adults assume within group interactions.

Adult Learners: Roles People Play

A graduate student in education recalls the major impact on him of the classic text by Schmuck and Schmuck (1997), *Group Processes in the Classroom,* in which the authors present revealing discussions about the various roles learners play as they participate and become accepted and contributing members of various small groups. These roles seem to apply to the adult learner as well.

To examine the idea of small groups a bit more closely, consider the number and kinds of formal and informal small groups with which adults are involved. Informal groups include the bridge club, the golf foursome, the carpool, the exercise class at Curves, the Cub's Fan Club, the poker game guys, the volleyball team, the dog show people, and family events. These are just a few examples of the little gatherings that adult learners attend and participate in regularly.

Adults also often interact with more formal small groups: school boards, faculty meetings, parent-teacher associations, community committees, department and/or grade level meetings, corporate seminars, graduations, award ceremonies, legal proceedings, and various and sundry institutional meetings and conferences.

As adult learners immerse themselves in these intellectual and social activities, they tend to take on specific and definitive roles in the group. Each becomes known for the role(s) that comes to them naturally. Someone usually takes on the role of caretaker or nurturer, another assumes the role of the devil's advocate, and still another plays the role of sage.

Someone usually takes on the role of caretaker.

Some roles are helpful and necessary to move the group forward, whereas others—most likely considered the negative roles—tend to consume time and negate any real progress for the group. For whatever reason, these seemingly unhelpful roles frequently emerge as part of the small-group process. Regardless of the circumstances, many of these roles turn up in small-group settings. In fact, if one of the members leaves the group either permanently or temporarily, someone else steps in to take over the absented role.

In a subsequent discussion, various roles that have been observed and documented by the authors and experts are described and delineated in some detail (Box 2.5). It is suggested that readers mentally try to slot these roles into their own real-world situations. It is expected that adults reading this piece will have a sense of déjà vu as they encounter numerous personalities and match them to their lives. In addition, the exercise provides incredible insights into the dynamics of small-group interactions, reactions, and eventual actions.

Cast of Characters

1. Caretaker	7. Negotiator
2. Know-It-All	8. Overachiever
3. Hitchhiker	9. Parliamentarian
4. Blocker (devil's advocate)	10. Sage
	11. Clown
5. Omnivore	12. Other
6. Inquisitor	

Box 2.5

Caretaker

Naturally, the caretaker role involves the nurturing and looking after of the others in the group. The Caretaker checks the temperature of the team with queries such as, "Do we need a little break?" "Is it time to wrap this up and continue when we are fresh?" Or, "Is everyone comfortable with this agenda (schedule or decision)?" The Caretaker plays a vital role in the group's wellness, which in turn subsequently affects the outcomes of the group. Florence Nightingale reincarnated, the Caretaker is the ultimate nurse at her best.

Know-It-All

This is the role of the pseudoexpert, not that of the authentic sage. The Know-It-All possesses a telling comment for every idea and is more than willing to share it. This person can monopolize the group and absorb gobs of time because he or she feels obliged to share every scrap of information with others. When the role player is discovered and recognized for what he or she is, team members tune out with an impending launch of the Know-It-All's rhetoric. The group eventually closes its ears to the Know-It-All's incessant preaching and pontificating, but the Know-It-All still poses a difficult challenge for facilitators who must handle this person with skill and finesse.

Hitchhiker

As the name implies, the Hitchhiker is someone who wants and accepts a free ride. The Hitchhiker contributes little or nothing to the group, so it soon learns not to look his or her way for any substantive contributions, leaving the Hitchhiker to become a silent passenger in the "vehicle" of himself. Often a passive learner and docile thinker who appears fairly removed from the action, he or she assumes this position because it seems to be part of this learner's demeanor, not to fulfill any need of the group.

Blocker (Devil's Advocate)

The blocker role is sometimes referred to in small groups as the "Devil's Advocate." This person tends to take contrary positions in the discussion and frequently apologizes for the interruption but insists that he or she has a cogent point that needs to be voiced. More often than not, these insertions tend to sideline the main discussion and may even cause untimely delays in the meeting agenda. Yet, there are times when the Devil's Advocate, rather than blocking the decision, brings up an important point that leads to a needed compromise to get everyone on board with the final stance.

The blocker role is sometimes referred to in small groups as the "Devil's Advocate."

Omnivore

Bruce Joyce and Beverly Showers (1995) often refer to the motivated adult learner as the "Omnivore"—the one who devours everything and is not satisfied until he or she knows every last detail of the issues at hand. The Omnivore is the group's highly motivated eager beaver, often pursuing a point beyond the interest of others. Yet, this is an example of the adult learner who is often a pleasure to work with because she pushes the leader to be more comprehensive about some things.

Inquisitor

The Inquisitor not only constantly asks questions but also frequently acts more like a key player in the "inquisition." While some of her questions may be to the point and relevant, others go over the top. The Inquisitor asks such things as, "How many?" "How much?" "When and where?" "What's the timeline for this?" "How many of us want to make this commitment?" "Is there a better plan that we haven't thought of yet?" "How does this compare to last year?" Although some of these questions address authentic issues harbored by other members of a "silent majority," others appear rather meaningless to many others in the group.

Negotiator

There is always a negotiator who takes on the role of bargaining for the group. This is the persistent person who negotiates meeting times, a lesser amount of work due, the location of the next meeting, or even the length of lunch break. This is the "professional negotiator" who knows just when and how to word the request so that the leader(s) must stop everything and show thoughtful consideration to the "reasonable" request. However, these requests often are out of context to what is going on at the moment and tend to create sidebars to the action at hand.

Note: a perfect corollary to this discussion on the cast of characters is the children's book by Doreen Cronin (2000) called *Click, Clack, Moo: Cows That Type.* In this delightful tale of farm animals, the role of negotiation is made crystal clear. Although an illustrated picture book for younger readers, its subtle message is almost more appropriate for adult learners.

Overachiever

The Overachiever is similar to but different from the Omnivore. Although both are motivated learners, the focus for the Omnivore is getting information during the input stage, while the focus for the Overachiever is in the output stage of giving information. The Overachiever goes into full swing when the assignments are due. He or she puts tremendous effort into the assigned tasks and goes above and beyond the call of duty in submitting comprehensive and superior products. The Overachiever feels a sense of accomplishment as he or she individually tackles a piece of the puzzle for the group.

> *The Overachiever feels a sense of accomplishment as he or she individually tackles a piece of the puzzle for the group.*

Parliamentarian

The Parliamentarian keeps the group on track with his or her frequent "calls to order." This role embraces the activities of the "policy police," as the role player insists on law and order or, at least, *Robert's Rules of Order.* The Parliamentarian demands a faithful following of the procedures of order—the rules and regulations and the acknowledged forms and norms set and accepted by the group. He or she is as interested in the *process* as in the *progress* of the product. This person is in it for the journey, not merely the destination, often asking such questions as, "Didn't we agree to vote after all the ideas have been fully explained?" "Haven't we extended our rule about time limits for members to present their case?" "I'd like to propose that we review the procedure we agreed to last time."

Sage

The Sage is the master or mentor of the group. This person garners the role for him- or herself, or, more likely, the team benevolently bestows the role of Sage on this deserving person. The Sage holds both formal and informal power, controlling discussion by simply withholding opinions or not giving the informal nod of agreement or look of consensus. In a more formal action, the Sage may approve or disapprove an idea with or without justification. The Sage, by nature, holds an enormous amount of power. A Sage may be a seasoned and experienced member of the group or the person who is most qualified, certified, or holds the highest degree or title. Again, this is a role that greatly influences the work of the group. Many times and in many cases, the Sage has the last word.

The Clown

Although the Clown may seem to play a frivolous role that groups can do without, this position is actually critical to a group's ongoing success. The Clown supplies the needed levity to diffuse a mounting conflict, skillfully providing a timely remark or a telling wisecrack that frequently brings emotions back down to a neutral level. In fact, the group counts on the Clown to monitor tight situations and intercede when emotions get too high or when anger, sarcasm, and cynicism begin to threaten group process. The Clown acts almost like an informal referee or umpire, checking the tenor of the group and interceding when necessary. Of course, the Clown may overplay his role and get on the nerves of other group members, but, in the end, the Clown offers humor, a welcome medicine for any team.

> *The Clown acts almost like an informal referee or umpire, checking the tenor of the group and interceding when necessary.*

In Summary

In summary, adults constitute a very special breed of learner, deserving the respect and attention of all whose work is linked to theirs. No longer children, the natural inhabitants of the teaching-learning environment, they are, rather, mature colleagues who bring great richness to the learning setting. Adult learners deserve respect, and, yes, reverence, for the hard work and heartfelt contributions they bring to their learning journeys. Adult learners underscore the adage that learning lasts through life.

To find more answers to the who, what, when, where, and why of the adult learner, another look at Zemke and Zemke (1995) seems appropriate. Revolving around the (1) motivation, (2) curriculum, and (3) classroom instruction of the adult learner, their research provides three useful categories on which to focus our understanding of why adults learn and how best to meet their needs.

Motivation to Learn (Reasons—the Why)

What motivates adult learners? Why do they enter into formal learning situations? What keeps adults aligned to learning and moving forward? These are the foundational concerns of those working with the adult learner.

Adults seek additional learning to cope with life-changing events or, in some cases, for its own reward. However, while these voluntary learners are pragmatic and self-directed in their approach to education, they don't always easily transfer ideas and skills into their work settings. In addition, although as busy adults they expect their class time to be compelling and useful, it is also common knowledge that adults are compelled to let their schoolwork take a backseat to family and jobs.

Curricular Designs (Content—the What)

What kinds of curricular designs are most inviting to adult learners? What catches their interest and how do these models translate into engaging adult curriculum? What should be key components in designing course work?

Adults prefer real-world exercises that focus on problem-centered learning scenarios. They prefer single-concept classes that go deep into an idea, preferring them over, say, survey courses that merely skim the surface of many variables. In fact, adult learners want a scaffolded design that allows them to understand how to complete a task, skill, or project. However, adults are not quick to discard old products or procedures. In fact, they do not want to use new materials until they are reassured through personal experience that the new materials are just as good or better than the former ones. Once they are convinced of the worth of the new models, however, they champion the cause with gusto.

Classroom Instruction (Delivery—the How)

What are the preferred methods in the classroom for adult learners? How do they want to learn? What instructional strategies work best with them?

First and foremost, because adult learners carry around reservoirs of personal experiences, they want to be honored among their colleagues as knowledgeable. For these reasons, an eclectic approach with an emphasis on "how-to" training works best with adults learners. While nonhuman learning (books, TV, Internet) is popular, in the classroom, group facilitation works better than lecture formats. Contrary to popular opinion, adults do not prefer "sit and git" instructional approaches, preferring to collaborate with others rather than learn alone.

To summarize, the adult is a self-directed learner, motivated by the circumstances of his or her life. A voluntary learner, he or she is pragmatic in outlook and demanding of reasonable and applicable learning. The adult learner is definitely a complex creature to teach, yet the rewards of doing so are real and tangible, as adults continue to move along their chosen paths.

TOOLS TO USE ■

1. Agree/Disagree: Things We Know

At this point, readers may want to perform a short exercise. Use your prior knowledge to evaluate the 20 statements in Box 2.6. After working through the set of statements, discuss the ideas with a colleague to see if there is a match. Then, after due diligence, turn to the end of the chapter, read the discussion of each of the 20 statements, and think about the implications of each.

Picturing the Adult Learner

I agree or disagree with these statements:

1. Adults seek learning experiences to cope with life-changing events.
2. For adults, learning is its own reward.
3. Adults prefer survey courses to single-concept classes.
4. Adults want to use new materials.
5. Adults are quick to reevaluate old material.
6. Adults prefer to learn alone.
7. Adults prefer to "sit and git."
8. Adults prefer "how-to" trainings.
9. An eclectic approach works best with adults.
10. Nonhuman learning (books, TV) is popular in adult learning.
11. Adults don't like problem-centered learning.
12. Adults carry reservoirs of personal experiences.
13. Real-world exercises are preferred.
14. Adults let their schoolwork take second seat to jobs and family.
15. Adults transfer ideas and skills easily into their work setting.
16. Adults are self-directed learners.
17. Facilitation of groups works better than lecture formats with adults.
18. Adults expect their class time to be well spent.
19. Adult learners are voluntary, self-directed learners.
20. Adults are pragmatic learners.

Box 2.6

SOURCES: Knowles, 1973; Zemke & Zemke, 1995

Discussion of Agree/Disagree Statements

Question 1: Adults seek learning experiences to cope with specific life-changing events. (True)

Discussion: Yes, this is true. Adult learners will seek learning opportunities in order to cope with job-related changes such as a promotion. They will seek new learning when stressed by changing family situations including divorce, a move, or an impending parent-care situation.

Case in Point: A professor once said, in a matter-of-fact way, "Ninety percent of female doctoral students are in a divorce or are newly divorced." That makes this point succinctly. Adults do seek learning to cope with major changes or disruptions in their lives.

Question 2: For adults, learning is its own reward. (True and False)

Discussion: True: Adults do learning for its own sake in areas of self-selected hobbies and interests. *False:* However, this may be a false statement in terms of learning for, or on, the job. Adults seek to learn because there is an impending need to proceed along their chosen career paths. In the sense of seeking job learning for its own sake, the answer is not true.

Case in point: Adults will pursue pleasurable learning to support their lifestyle and to become more skillful as a gardener, needle pointer, artist, gourmet cook, musician, or even day trader. Yet most learning for adults that is job related is not done for its own reward but rather because it is needed for advancement or maintaining the current job.

Question 3: Adults prefer survey courses to single-concept courses. (False)

Discussion: The statement is false. Adult learners prefer to learn something in depth rather than at a superficial, introductory, or awareness level.

They want to delve into the specifics of the learning with depth and understanding. They do not like to skim the surface generalities. They want specifics.

Case in point: Adults want to pursue particular software training such as Excel rather than take a general course on office software.

Question 4: Adults want to use new materials. (False)

Discussion: Not so! Adult learners prefer the tried and true. They are frequently reluctant to switch to new materials, whether new software, new hardware, or new ideas. Adult learners epitomize two sayings: "It's hard to teach an old dog new tricks," and "You can lead a horse to water, but you can't make him drink."

Case in point: Adults like the old comfortable shoes! They may come to the training to learn about the new information, but that doesn't mean they will actually embrace it or put it into practice.

Question 5: Adults are quick to reevaluate old materials. (False)

Discussion: Paralleling the previous statement, adults do not easily give up the old materials. They tend to hang on to them and continue to use them when they can. If they are forced to move into the new material, they may still retain much of the old, or they gradually and cautiously weave the new into their existing repertoire. It is usually a slow process in which adult learners eventually achieve a level of confidence that allows them to move forward.

Case in point: Textbook adoptions cause great concern for teachers. They do not want to give up their well-worn units or their favorite activities. Turning to the humorous for an example, the executive of a small publishing company in an attempt to get everyone computer literate banned the use of typewriters in the office. Although the office team followed orders *on the surface,* the entire staff conspired to keep a lone typewriter in the storeroom for "emergencies." In their mind, emergencies occurred every time someone needed to type an address on an envelope, a skill they had not yet conquered on the computer.

Question 6: Adults prefer to learn alone. (False)

Discussion: Nope! Adults like working with others. They thrive in collaboration with a colleague and in the dialogue process that ensues. Adult learners become quite reflective as learning partners or learning teams.

Case in point: Most distance learning models are designed with a collaborative component so adult learners can dialogue with a buddy or partner and feel a sense of support.

Question 7: Adults prefer "sit and gits." (False)

Discussion: Adult learners want a collaborative, interactive, hands-on learning experience. They want to try things in step-by-step procedural ways. Adults are eager to do whatever it is they are learning to do, and they want to try it out with an expert nearby.

Case in point: A friend attended a software training that was conducted in a hotel ballroom with 450 people in attendance. No one had a computer to use except the instructor, who projected the performance sequence on a 12 × 12 screen. My friend's appraisal of the experience was, "It was the worst seminar I have ever attended."

Question 8: Adults prefer "how-to" trainings. (True)

Discussion: Absolutely! Adult learners want the nuts and bolts! They want to know specifically *how to* manage the task or skill they are learning. Adult learners are eager to know all about the practical components so that they can practice them and take them back to their work setting with ease and grace.

Case in point: When learning to play golf, the novice does not really care that much about the history of the game itself, about the metaphors, the equipment, or the rules. They want to know how to grip the club, which club to use, and how.

Question 9: An eclectic approach works best with the adult learner. (True)

Discussion: Yes! Focus groups often reveal preferences of adult learners that include a combination of online and Web-based and the more traditional face-to-face interactions.

Case in point: Many field-based or distance learning programs in education require intermittent on-site retreats, either over a weekend or during the summer holidays. In this way, they can meet the needs of those who want some face to face.

Question 10: Nonhuman learning (books, TV, Internet) is popular in adult learning. (True)

Discussion: Although adult learners relish collaboration and face-to-face dialogue, they also, at times, embrace nonhuman forms of learning. Books, television, and the Internet are popular sources of information for adult learners.

> Books, television, and the Internet are popular sources of information for adult learners.

Case in point: Adult viewers cite *Band of Brothers,* an eight-part docudrama on HBO about WWII, as the greatest tool for clarifying the historical event.

Question 11: Adults don't like problem-centered learning. (False)

Discussion: No! Just the opposite is true. Adults are hooked into learning situations through the skill of appropriate and personally relevant real-world problems. By presenting scenarios of actual situations, adult learners are attracted to the problem and immediately get into problem-solving mode.

Case in point: The vignettes of schools in case studies provide fertile ground for leadership seminars during which practical problem solving becomes the rule, resulting in rich discussions.

Question 12: Adults carry reservoirs of personal experience. (True)

Discussion: So true! Adult learners are laden with myriad experiences that they bring to the learning setting. In fact, the expression "lesson learned" is critical to the learning process. As new information comes in, adult brains search for patterns that fit. By attaching the new to former or existing information, adult learners actually internalize the learning for storage in long-term memory. Adult learners tend to pursue learning along the lines of career interests that will eventually translate into job advancement or life fulfillment. Thus, adult learners are often building on an existing knowledge base that can be both rich and diverse.

Case in point: An estate-planning attorney seeks accounting and tax seminars that can continue to build and update her knowledge base for her primary business in estate planning.

Question 13: Real-world exercises are preferred. (True)

Discussion: This is true. Adult learners want actual situations to ponder and problems to solve. They do not especially like the "fantasy" problems as evidenced by their reluctance to dig in with this kind of problem; instead, they turn off.

Case in point: Middle school teachers will complain, "But this is not realistic. This would never happen. It's not useful to spend time on these hypothetical situations. No school schedule allows for this kind of time for 'advisory programs.'"

Question 14: Adults let their schoolwork take second place to jobs and family. (True)

Discussion: The bad news is yes, they do. The good news is they do it because they are clear about their responsibilities. But because they see learning as part of those responsibilities, their schoolwork does get done, too.

Case in point: Many a mom spends quality time and energy with family affairs, including errands, soccer practice, dinner, and housework before they settle down, late in the evening, to the reading required for their graduate classes.

Question 15: Adults transfer ideas and skills easily into their work settings. (False)

Discussion: Adults do not always see the application to their work. When the learning is closely related to work in the case of a newly learned skill, only then is the transfer ready-made. More often than not, with complex processes, transfer requires explicit coaching and much "shepherding" to be skillfully applied.

Case in point: Adults usually can move between a PC and a Mac computer with little effort. Yet they may experience great difficulty in changing from one operating system to another. The operating systems are often conceptually quite different; therefore, the transfer must be more mindful.

Question 16: Adults are self-directed learners. (True)

Discussion: True! True! Adults are usually clear and focused about what they want to achieve. They select the right program for themselves to meet their specific goals in terms of time constraints, effort, and outcomes.

Case in point: Second-career teachers seek out an expedient university program that offers the course work needed, the necessary practicum, and the alternative certification required to actually be placed in a school for a teaching position.

Question 17: Facilitation of groups works better than lecture format with adult learners. (True)

Discussion: Adults want to experience learning with real and authentic activities. They want to collaborate and discuss their work and form reasoned judgments about how they are doing. For adults, working in groups gives them a chance to dialogue with other learners to confirm understanding and to discuss process.

Case in point: A well-run training session at a local bank involves the participants in case study scenarios as it teaches customer service skills.

Question 18: Adults expect their class time to be well spent. (True)

Discussion: An adamant yes! Time is precious! Adults do not want their valuable time wasted in inefficient or superfluous ways. They are committed to a certain amount of time for class, and they want it to be well spent.

Case in point: One graduate student habitually complained to a professor who regularly dismissed the class early, while the undergraduates were ecstatic! The adult learner wanted to get everything he could possibly get in his time with the teacher.

Question 19: Adults are voluntary, self-directed learners. (True)

Discussion: Yes, in many cases adults seek learning situations they want or need and voluntarily attend to their school responsibilities. Yet, in some cases, they are volunteering only to fill a requirement for certification or advancement.

Case in point: A golf pro voluntarily attends the required hours of PGA classes needed annually to retain certain levels of certification.

Question 20: Adults are pragmatic learners. (True)

Discussion: Oh, yes! The picture by now, after 19 previously discussed traits, is becoming quite clear. Adult learners are learning for a reason. They are focused, tenacious, and goal oriented. Adult learners want to cross the finish line and go on with their lives!

Case in point: Many adult learners accelerate their doctoral programs and complete the course work in record time. They are eager to get on with the real work—the dissertation.

2. Role Play: True Confessions . . . The Role I Often Play

Using the cast of characters section in this chapter, try to apply these ideas by reviewing the list and trying a few of the most obvious labels on members of your group. It is also recommended by the authors that the cast of characters be discussed within groups. Just the awareness of these roles offers insights and discoveries about the group and how it does its best work.

3. Adult Learner—Tiny Transfer Book

Adult learner is. . . Adult learner wants . . . Adult learner prefers . . . Adult learner brings . . .

Adult learner is . . . Adult learner wants . . . Adult learner prefers . . . Adult learner brings . . .

Create a tiny transfer book and summarize your thoughts about the adult learner using these categorical headings (see Box 6.6, page 103).

Instructions

Add three comments under each one. For example, The adult learner is . . .

1. Pragmatic
2. Voluntary
3. Self-directed

3

A Guide to Site-Based Professional Development

Vignette: Historical View

After 20 years in the field, there are some things that are known about professional development—things known about the evolution of professional development models, the value of building learning organizations, the elements of sound professional development, and the critical components of effective training models.

To begin, one can follow the evolution of professional development models from "the institute day" through districtwide professional development plans and site-based professional development to the building of communities of learners and individualized professional learning.

EVOLUTION OF PROFESSIONAL DEVELOPMENT ■

The Institute Day

Historically, a common model of professional development was the one-day presentation. Sometimes referred to as a "dog and pony show," this model is often a presentation made by an expert or a team of experts. The one—and only—redeeming quality of one-shot programs is as an awareness session to initiate an innovation. Following the awareness, an interested cadre of learners is culled from the larger group for further professional development.

The institute day is designed as a smorgasbord of offerings.

In another historic model, the institute day is designed as a smorgasbord of offerings, with teachers selecting their sessions, far in advance, and traveling around the district to their chosen session. This model has more appeal than the one-shot deal because of the options, but it is still a dog-and-pony-show kind of day, lacking the follow-up of more comprehensive models.

Districtwide Professional Development Plan

A districtwide professional development plan is a model that evolved in the early days of staff development because it was a natural way to introduce an entire faculty to an innovation. This model is sometimes referred to as the "spray paint method" or as some have said, "Spray and pray." Everyone has cooperative learning training. The entire district is exposed to the theory of learning styles. Although this method works better than the one-shot deal because it usually involves multiple days over periods of time, it is still not sufficient training for full implementation without the key ingredients of practice and coaching.

Well-designed strategic planning for ongoing, continuous professional development is the hallmark of excellence in districts that target increased student achievement. These plans are constructed with input from all the stakeholders and may be part of the district package for state and federal funding. Programs of excellence are job-embedded models, sustained over time, with practice and coaching as integral elements.

Site-Based Professional Development

The concept of site-based professional development is training at the building level and is designed to be more responsive to schoolwide goals that impact the whole staff. Effective site-based staff development operates within the parameters of an established, long-term staff development plan that often is filed at the district and state level. The strategic plan includes various innovations that often lead to both the general overall goals of the district and those that are specific to the school and its particular demographics and needs. The strategic plan model can be among the best when the leadership understands the facilitation processes of setting goals, obtaining buy-in by stakeholders, and building a community of learners.

The drawback to this model is funding—a single school has a small budget. Often several schools collaborate to create the needed funds for initiatives.

Communities of Learners

Promoted throughout the literature (Fullan, 1982; Goodlad, 1983; Guskey, 2000; Joyce & Showers, 1983, 1995, 2002; Little, 1975; Schmoker, 1996), the concept of collaborative teams reigns supreme in today's climate for professional learning. Grade level teams, department teams, core middle level teams, literacy or math teams, and data teams are alive and well in the school setting. These collaborative groupings serve to customize the professional learning to relevant, purposeful learning

> *Teams often become quite self-directed and resourceful as they address urgent and real concerns and find professional development solutions that speak directly to them.*

opportunities in which the transfer and application are directly aligned to the people and their specific work settings. These smallish groups of teachers find common ground for data discussions, book studies, debriefings, instructional interventions, and the examination of student work for patterns and trends that focus instructional time. In fact, the power of the collaborations is such that teams often become quite self-directed and resourceful as they address urgent and real concerns and find professional development solutions that speak directly to them. Some believe that the impact of this kind of cooperation, with continued, ongoing, highly relevant discussions is the key to lasting change in the schools.

Individualized Professional Learning Plans

As a distinctive and fairly contemporary practice, individual professional learning plans are becoming the norm in many school districts, as more states incorporate recertification requirements. In this model, each staff member is expected to plot a course of professional development opportunities, comprised of a specified number of clock hours and/or graduate credits that lead to state requirements for recertification. These opportunities range from traditional workshops to graduate course work to mentoring responsibilities to action research in the classroom. Although approval of the professional development experiences remains at the district level, the individual teacher devises the actual plan with input, suggestions, and guidance from supervisory personnel. This model can be customized to the wants and needs of the individual as he or she determines an appropriate career path. The individualized plan becomes a package of growth and development tailored suitably to the talents and skills of the individual person. This plan offers a wide range of choices, but there is an expectation for rigor and relevance in the selections made.

Summary

To summarize, professional development in a district often is comprised of all five described models. Yet, to have a program of integrity, strategic and long-term planning is always necessary. Districts are now beginning to work with systemic plans in place for professional development.

Best Practices in Professional Development

It seems viable to begin a piece of information on why traditional professional development often does not work. Lieberman (1988) writes about schools as learning organizations in which professional development is an integral part of everything that goes on in the school. In her discussion of effective models of learning organizations, she delineates the reasons why professional development often fails in its mission. The ten reasons, depicted in Box 3.1, provide clear clues to some of the limitations that impede change through professional development practices.

Reasons Why Professional Development Fails

1. Lack of knowledge about how teachers learn

2. Teachers' definition of the problems of practice ignored

3. Agenda for reform not part of teachers' professional learning

4. Teaching described as set of technical skills, not invention

5. Importance of context within which teachers work is ignored

6. Support mechanisms and learning over time not considered

7. Time and mechanism for inventing often absent

8. Importance of facilitating at school level to change practice absent

9. Connection to school culture to change practice often ignored

10. Networks to support change in practice not promoted

Box 3.1

In summary, the ten limitations cluster around the idea of lack of input on the part of key stakeholders, the teachers; initiatives introduced without sufficient context; and teacher creativity not considered as part of the process.

At the same time, Box 3.1 provides insight into the power of learning communities. When educators know how teachers learn, when to involve them in generating the alternatives, when to foster creative solutions, and when to support them within the culture and the context of their work, the resulting response is positive and long lasting. In fact, that is how real change occurs—over time and with the ownership of all directly involved.

That is how real change occurs—over time and with the ownership of all directly involved.

As the field of professional development matures, the literature is filled with findings about what is and is not effective in working with the adult learner. Among the many elements discussed in myriad journal articles and emerging research studies, there are seven critical components that seem to spell success for substantive, long lasting change. These seven professional development attributes

> *These seven professional development attributes appear repeatedly in the literature.*

appear repeatedly in the literature and are supported by leading voices in this area of study. The following seven adjectives describe rich, robust, and rigorous models of professional learning (Box 3.2): sustained, job embedded, collegial, interactive, integrated, results oriented, and practical.

Professional Development: Seven Critical Qualities

1. Sustained: Training is implemented over time.

2. Job embedded: Training occurs and/or continues at the work site.

3. Collegial: Training builds and supports a community of learners.

4. Interactive: Training invites, involves, and engages participants.

5. Integrated: Training is eclectic (Web-based, online, text, face-to-face).

6. Results oriented: Training meets a need, is goal driven, is data driven.

7. Practical, hands on: Training is relevant with real-world problems.

Box 3.2

A more detailed discussion is warranted. What does each of these qualities contribute? What does it look and sound like to design skillful and sound professional development? How are the seven elements related to each other and the overall effectiveness of the process? To elaborate on the seven qualities, each is defined with synonyms and described operationally through T-chart graphics to depict what they actually look and sound like.

Sustained

Sustained (Figure 3.1) means that the professional development is ongoing and continual. It is a process that evolves over sufficient time for the participants to become acquainted with the basic ideas and to have time to work with the ideas in authentic and relevant ways and with the support of supervisory staff and colleagues.

Figure 3.1   Sustained Professional Development

Looks Like	Sounds Like
Yearlong or multiyear initiative	"It will be offered again."
Schoolwide and/or districtwide initiative	"We are starting with the freshman program and will proceed through Grades 10–12 programs, adding a grade each year."

Job Embedded

Although the introductory sessions of the professional development experience may involve a centralized presentation at the district office, an integral part of the plan includes on-site, guided, and independent practice, supported by effective coaching and regular and specific feedback. In fact, job-embedded (Figure 3.2) practice, rehearsal, and repetition of the skills and strategies in the classroom are critical to the overall success of the innovation.

Figure 3.2   Job-Embedded Professional Development

Looks Like	Sounds Like
Classroom application of skills	"Your application was appropriate."
Peers coaching each other's work	"It worked well, but it needs better pacing."
Teachers observing each other	"I think that was the most effective part."

Collegial

Collegial models (Figure 3.3) of professional development build on the concept of learning communities that bond in trusting relationships. Colleagues rely on each other and take on the roles of coach and cheerleader for the friends they are working with. Collegiality is what bonds the group of learners. It provides the emotional support for change as well as the expertise for developing the skills.

Colleagues rely on each other and take on the roles of coach and cheerleader.

Interactive

Interactive professional development (Figure 3.4) demonstrates the skillfulness of an effective facilitator who knows how to invite participants

Figure 3.3   Collegial Professional Development

Looks Like	Sounds Like
Team meeting	Laughter, teaching, and joking around
Friends helping friends	"I'll do that part."
Shared project or product	"I could never have done this without your help."
Informal gatherings	"It's been so helpful to have a partner."

Figure 3.4   Interactive Professional Development

Looks Like	Sounds Like
Research on the Web	"I love the chat room."
Classroom briefings	"I like the virtual office hours."
Buying used texts	"I submitted my paper online."

to become involved and, sometimes, deeply engaged in the experience. This interactive model of adult learning features the leader in the critical role of "guide on the side," with participants working collaboratively in pairs or in small groups.

Integrated

Integrated models of professional development are multimodal models that dictate an eclectic approach to adult learning. The experience might include Web-based learning, online interactions, traditional actions, text formats, or face-to-face instruction but will usually use myriad approaches that appeal to diverse adult learning. As do young learners, adult learners need diversity and multimodal approaches. Each brain is different. Each responds to different stimuli.

Results Oriented

Results-oriented professional development (Figure 3.5) addresses an identified need that is often data driven. For example, disaggregated subskills demonstrate a deficit area in higher-order thinking skills.

Results-oriented professional development is goal driven.

Figure 3.5   Results-Oriented Professional Development

Looks Like	Sounds Like
Data charts	"Let's check our progress."
Written goals	"We're close to meeting the goal."
Visuals with steps and benchmarks	"This intervention needs adjustments."

Results-oriented professional development is goal driven. The target performances are delineated and clearly articulated to all stakeholders. Everyone knows what the target goal is and the steps needed to get to that goal. Benchmarks are measured along the way to track progress and to keep the goal clearly in mind.

Practical

Practical professional development (Figure 3.6) takes the theory and makes it real. In essence, it operationalizes the theory and turns the learning into relevant, real-world learning by creating scenarios and problems to solve. Practical learning makes it clear to the learner how the learning helps address authentic situations that one might face every day. Practical learning takes the conceptual situation and transforms it into a hands-on learning experience that has immediate applications built into it.

> Practical professional development (Figure 3.6) takes the theory and makes it real.

Figure 3.6   Practical Professional Development

Looks Like	Sounds Like
Authentic scenario	"You are a stakeholder . . . ."
Hands-on problem solving	"What are the facts we know and need to know?"
Real-world problem	"How does this work?"

In summary, these seven elements make the difference between professional development that works and professional development that fails. In the successful plan of professional development, meaningful applications are evident and effective. The results are long lasting, with continuing impact on student achievement. In the unsuccessful plan, the professional development often is a one-shot deal or a dog and pony show that is never actually applied and which results in, at best, spotty applications that are short-lived. The results in terms of student achievement are nonexistent or highly elusive. Thus, following the recognized design and including the elements that have emerged from the literature seems to be the logical choice for developing professional development plans.

Research Base for Professional Development

Most Powerful School Improvement Tool

In a similar vein, Schmoker (1996) advocates learning communities that are fairly flexible and informal but fiercely effective. He believes that the teacher team is the most powerful school improvement tool schools have. Schmoker believes that when teachers put their heads together and focus on an impending concern, uncovered and/or supported by data, they will find the best solutions because they are the ones closest to and most invested in the problem. Inherent in his writings is the concept of data-driven decisions for instruction and then, in turn, for the professional development needed to effectively implement the instructional decision. His model has three parts, as listed in Box 3.3.

> *Schmoker (1996) advocates learning communities that are fairly flexible and informal but fiercely effective.*

Schmoker's School Improvement Model

- Managed data (Data): Student achievement data; demographics
- Meaningful teams (Dialogue): Grade level/department/vertical/core teams
- Measurable goals (Decision): Instructional/professional development goals

---

Box 3.3

Briefly, this streamlined model consists of forming a team of teachers who work with the same group of students (creating meaningful teams). When formed, the team focuses on the most urgent achievement concerns revealed from ongoing assessment data (data, dialogue phases). Then, based on the data, the ongoing professional dialogue, and the expertise of the team, goals (smart goals—specific, measurable, attainable, results-oriented, time-bound) are set, interventions are planned, and the plan is put into action (decision phase). Often the instructional intervention requires specific professional development before the teachers are ready to fully implement the intervention. The entire process of data, dialogue, and decisions is a clear and simple methodology for school improvement, which works because the goal-setting phase is focused on results. This model is delineated more fully in the book, *Data! Dialogue! Decisions! The Data Difference* (Pete & Sambo, 2004).

Research Summary of Findings on Professional Development

Joyce and Showers's (1983, 1995, 2002) work in the field of staff development has yielded a body of knowledge that summarizes what is known and most effective in terms of professional development training and sustaining change in schools. Their ideas are delineated in Box 3.4. In short, the researchers have found that there are four critical elements to the training model that include theory, demonstration, practice, and coaching. More detailed discussions of these four elements of training appear in Chapter **8**.

The Training Model

Include THEORY	0% transfer in the classroom
And, add a DEMONSTRATION	0% transfer in the classroom
And, provide PRACTICE	0% transfer in the classroom
And, require on-site COACHING	95% transfer in the classroom

Box 3.4

SOURCE: Joyce and Showers, 2002.

In addition to understandings about the most effective training models, the researchers Joyce and Showers have accumulated information about the adult learner and the impact of training on various profiles of teachers. Their findings offer a clear and concise reading of what is known about how professional development influences a faculty or individual teachers. The summary of the research on professional development is revealing. It is summarized in Box 3.5.

National Staff Development Standards

The quintessential organization for staff developers is the National Staff Development Council (NSDC) headquartered in Oxford, Ohio. This national group has affiliations in many states. Together, they set the standards for sound professional learning experiences for the academic communities of schools. Box 3.6 presents a brief listing of the NSDC standards divided into three arenas: context standards, process standards, and content standards.

The quintessential organization for staff developers is the National Staff Development Council (NSDC).

Research on Professional Development

1. What the teacher thinks about teaching determines what the teacher does when teaching. In training teachers, therefore, we must provide more than "going through the motions" of teaching.

2. Almost all teachers can take useful information back to their classrooms when training includes three parts: (1) presentation of theory, (2) demonstration of the new strategy, and (3) initial practice in the workshop.

3. Teachers are likely to keep and use new strategies and concepts if they receive coaching (either expert or peer) while they are trying the new ideas in the classrooms.

4. Competent teachers with high self-esteem usually benefit more from training than their less competent, less confident colleagues.

5. Flexibility in thinking helps teachers learn new skills and incorporate them into their repertoires of tried-and-true methods.

6. Individual teaching styles and value orientations do not often affect teachers' abilities to learn from staff development.

7. A basic level of knowledge or skill in a new approach is necessary before teachers can buy into it.

8. Initial enthusiasm for training is reassuring to the organizers but has relatively little influence upon learning.

9. It doesn't seem to matter where or when training is held, and it doesn't really matter what the role of the trainer is (teacher, administrator, or professor). What does matter is the training design.

10. Similarly, the effects of training do not depend on whether teachers organize and direct the program, although social cohesion and shared understanding do facilitate teachers' willingness to try out new ideas.

These findings provide critical insights for the field of professional development that are integral to designing successful models.

Box 3.5

SOURCE: Joyce, B. et al. (1980) "Improving Inservice Training-Message to Research." *Educational Leadership 37*(5) p. 379. Reprinted by permission. The Association for Supervision for Supervision and Curriculum Development is a worldwide community of educators advocating sound policies and sharing best practices to achieve the success of each learner. To learn more, visit ASCD at www.ascd.org.

NSDC Professional Development Standards At-a-Glance

Context standards

Learning communities

Leadership

Adult learning

Process standards

Data driven

Evaluation multisources

Research-based strategies

Design appropriate

Human learning/change theory

Collaboration

Content Standards

Equity

Quality teaching

Family involvement

Box 3.6

SOURCE: Used with permission of the National Staff Development Council, www.nsdc.org.

Within the context standards, discussion turns to the advocacy of professional learning communities, leadership concerns, and a knowledge base about the adult learner.

Process standards include elements about data-driven professional development that aligns to meaningful instructional data in the school or district or evaluation issues, proven strategies, appropriate designs, change theory, human learning, and collaborations. Finally, the content standards address the issue of equity, quality teaching, and family involvement. To find out more within each strand, the standards are discussed more fully on the Web site: www.nsdc.org

Again, these standards attempt to define quality professional development (PD) for school districts and change agencies. The PD standards are a hallmark of PD in this decade. For more details, go to their Web site: www.nsdc.org.

Formats and Frameworks That Work

Everyone agrees! To keep teaching fresh, to provide constant opportunities for teachers to grow and develop, schools must have comprehensive professional development. But how do schools find the time and money to cultivate this community of learners among its teachers? This discussion presents 10 ways to find the time needed to renew teaching skills and the teaching spirit.

Everyone agrees! To keep teaching fresh . . . schools must have comprehensive professional development.

Community of Learners: Finding the Time

Once the community of learners is established, it flourishes. Renewal possibilities abound for teachers to engage in meaningful professional development experiences. Within this community structure, teachers study, learn, and reflect on the art and science of teaching. As they refine the skills of their craft, the collaborative, collegial process energizes their teaching and renews the spirit within.

There are many creative ways to find the time for teachers to learn.

But, how does one go about creating a community of learners? It takes a precious commodity: time. Fortunately, there are many creative ways to find the time for teachers to learn.

How does one find the time for busy, overscheduled, overburdened teachers to meet, talk, share, articulate, study, and reflect on the teaching/learning process? Here are some creative and varied ways (Box 3.7) schools have devised in ongoing efforts to find time for teachers to learn (Fogarty, 2001c).

- Purchase time in the summer or borrow time by shifting the school day.
- Create new time through teacher incentives.
- Tier time with existing functions such as lunch and early morning arrivals.
- Schedule common time for teachers to learn and capitalize on "found time" when a student teacher does her independent practice.
- Free up time for teachers through a parent volunteer corps or a senior citizen program.
- Reschedule time by radically revising the school calendar or simply using the existing time differently and planning carefully for scheduled release time.

Finding Time for Professional Development

Purchase time	Capitalize on found time
Borrow time	Free up time
Create new time	Reschedule time
Tier the time	Use time differently
Use common time	Schedule release time

Box 3.7

A closer look at these PD options reveals the creativity of schools to find time for the teacher to learn. These options represent actual examples in practice.

Purchase Time

Take advantage of teachers' summer hiatus when they're not on the front line with kids every day. Tap into their knowledge and experience by hiring teams of teachers to develop curriculum, district standards, units of study, or assessment instruments. Capitalize on their expertise and pay them to think, write, and create the materials that will sustain their teaching throughout the year.

Borrow Time

By adding 15 minutes a day to the beginning or end of the day, Monday through Thursday, the staff gains a total of one hour on Friday for professional development activities. Although this one hour each Friday may seem like too little time, think about the cumulative effect of 40 Fridays throughout the year. That is significant time.

Create New Time

Provide incentives such as lane changes on the salary schedule for graduate hours, alternative certifications, and advanced degrees. This existing policy, in practice in some districts, motivates staff to pursue self-directed professional development opportunities. In turn, a sense of efficacy prevails as teachers plot their own path of professional renewal.

Tier the Time

Picture the tiered wedding cake and imagine using the concept in designing professional development opportunities. Tier activities with existing functions that are already in place. Develop the idea of the "Lunch Bunch" on Thursdays, and offer a "tried-and-true strategy" for immediate classroom application.

Develop the idea of the "Lunch Bunch."

Tier an early-bird meeting with the required before-school time for teachers. For five or six weeks, schedule a meeting for early Thursday morning and call it the "Breakfast Club." Use the time for a book study group.

Use Common Time

Schedule a block of time for teacher teams to meet and work on curriculum units. This team time may be part of the block schedule structure that a whole school has adopted, or it might be simply a block of time carved out for the math team, the third grade team, or for a vertical team of sixth, seventh, and eighth grade teachers. It's a matter of deciding that this team planning time is a priority for quality instruction.

Capitalize on Found Time

Serendipitous times occasionally occur that offer opportunities for teachers to have some quality professional development experience. For example, when a student teacher is doing independent practice in the final few weeks, there might be a chunk of time for observing other teachers, for reading, or for researching some pertinent aspect of teaching or learning.

Free Up Time

Parent volunteers, senior citizens, and visiting artists sometimes create opportunities for a team of teachers to meet while another team supervises and complements the activity planned for the students. To create this scenario, some schools foster a volunteer program for parents, with one parent leader dedicated to scheduling the volunteer corps for appropriate activities. In this way, the school garners solid community involvement and support in natural ways that benefit all those involved.

Reschedule Time

Research, discuss, and plan the school year differently. Revise the calendar year to move toward the concept of year-round education or a professional development week at the end of the year or prior to the start of the term in the fall. With a radically revised annual calendar, many things are possible for student learning and for professional development. Also, think about the daily timetable and how it might be revamped for learning opportunities for students and staff.

> *Covet the actual time when people are face to face for matters that directly influence student learning.*

Use Time Differently

Rethink faculty and department meetings already on the schedule. Try to encourage the use of memos or e-mail for bulletins and announcements whenever possible. Save the department or faculty meeting for instructional issues, curriculum planning, or to examine standards and assessment issues. Covet the actual time when people are face to face for matters that directly influence student learning.

Schedule Release Time

Use the standard inservice, institute, and professional development days that are already part and parcel of most school calendars. Create long-range professional development plans from a shared vision with staff that dovetails with district goals. Implement short-term professional development experiences that provide staff opportunities to learn the skills needed to achieve the goals and to develop the spirit to carry them through. In this way, the time set aside for staff training serves to truly improve student learning.

■   **TOOLS TO USE**

1. Rate Your Professional Development Time

As you review the 10 opportunities (Box 3.8) presented in this discussion, think about the ones you already do, the ones you might want to adopt, and the ones you may need to adapt in some way to make them work in your school setting. In addition, think of combinations or entirely new ideas for the community of adult learners in your building to meet and keep their teaching fresh.

**Evaluating Ideas for Finding Time
for Professional Development**

*   Already Do
+   Adopt Idea as Is
?   Adapt Idea for Our Use
&   Combine

_____ Purchase time   _____ Capitalize on found time

_____ Borrow time   _____ Free up time

_____ Create new time   _____ Reschedule time

_____ Tier the time   _____ Use time differently

_____ Use common time   _____ Schedule release time

Box 3.8

Form 3.1   Tear/Share Activity Four Questions

1. It doesn't seem to matter if the training is top down or bottom up. Explain.	2. What are the two most important findings (in your opinion)?
3. Why might the training design matter most?	4. What is one significant of this research? implication

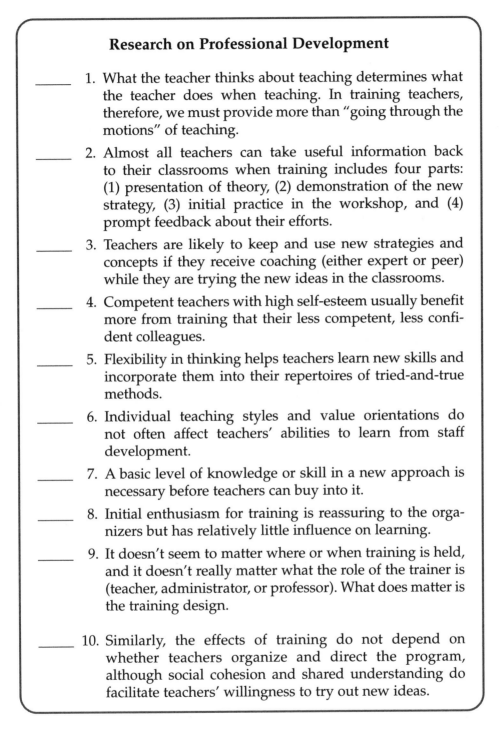

Research on Professional Development

_____ 1. What the teacher thinks about teaching determines what the teacher does when teaching. In training teachers, therefore, we must provide more than "going through the motions" of teaching.

_____ 2. Almost all teachers can take useful information back to their classrooms when training includes four parts: (1) presentation of theory, (2) demonstration of the new strategy, (3) initial practice in the workshop, and (4) prompt feedback about their efforts.

_____ 3. Teachers are likely to keep and use new strategies and concepts if they receive coaching (either expert or peer) while they are trying the new ideas in the classrooms.

_____ 4. Competent teachers with high self-esteem usually benefit more from training that their less competent, less confident colleagues.

_____ 5. Flexibility in thinking helps teachers learn new skills and incorporate them into their repertoires of tried-and-true methods.

_____ 6. Individual teaching styles and value orientations do not often affect teachers' abilities to learn from staff development.

_____ 7. A basic level of knowledge or skill in a new approach is necessary before teachers can buy into it.

_____ 8. Initial enthusiasm for training is reassuring to the organizers but has relatively little influence on learning.

_____ 9. It doesn't seem to matter where or when training is held, and it doesn't really matter what the role of the trainer is (teacher, administrator, or professor). What does matter is the training design.

_____ 10. Similarly, the effects of training do not depend on whether teachers organize and direct the program, although social cohesion and shared understanding do facilitate teachers' willingness to try out new ideas.

Box 3.9

SOURCE: Joyce, B. et al. (1980) "Improving Inservice Training-Message to Research." _Educational Leadership_ 37(5) p. 379. Reprinted by permission. The Association for Supervision for supervision and Curriculum Development is a worldwide community of educators advocating sound policies and sharing best practices to achieve the success of each learner. To learn more, visit ASCD at www.ascd.org.

2. Tear/Share Research

With three colleagues, form a team of four and try the following activity called "the cooperative tear/share":

- Step 1: "Read and Rank" all the items in the list in Box 3.8; top three, bottom three.
  Research on Professional Development by Joyce and Showers.
- Step 2: Teams of 4; count off 1–2—3–4; mark paper into 4 sections.
- Step 3: Each person responds to all four questions.
- Step 4: Tear apart sections 1–2—3–4 and give to person with the number.
- Step 5: Summarize (orally) the four responses for your number.

3. ABC Graffiti—Historical Look at Professional Development

Using every letter of the alphabet, brainstorm professional development ideas. Work alone or with a partner or team. Once completed, compare responses and discuss the striking ones. Then, write a summary statement of the element under study. For example:

Professional Development

A—Adult learner

B—Buddies

C—Collaborations

D—Data-Driven

Etc.

Summary statement (example): Professional development for the adult learner is collaborative and data driven.

4

A Guide to the Role of Designing Professional Learning

Vignette: Time to Kill

To tell a tale on a new consultant, imagine the scene in a city north of Detroit in Michigan. The district had committed to a well-designed professional development plan that extended over four days of training, spaced out over about two months' time. The lead consultant had completed the initial day of introductory material, setting the stage for a second day of hands-on work with 10 models for integrating the curricula. A fairly new consultant, but one fully trained in the models, was sent to do the day.

When the evaluations came back, participants gave rave reviews for the morning session. The comments for the afternoon, however, read somewhat differently, ranging from "Things seemed to drag" to "We could have done everything in a half-day session" to "The afternoon was something of a waste."

When we asked the consultant what happened, her reply was quite revealing about the importance of the training design and, in particular, the pacing of the training. She admitted, somewhat sheepishly, "We had a wonderfully productive morning, and I did everything that was planned. Somehow I managed to cover all the material in three hours. Then, after lunch, I had nothing really left to do, so I tried to fill in with some things, but it didn't seem to go over very well."

The lesson for this beginning staff developer? Overplan! No matter how well the plan is designed, sometimes the trainer covers things faster than expected. She learned, consequently, that she must always have a few more strategies that deepen or extend the learning.

■ DESIGNING ROLE

Description of the Role: Designer at the Site—Creating the Setting

According to Joyce and Showers (2002), the design of the training is what makes or breaks the effectiveness of the training. Thus the role of designer seems equally crucial to the overall process. Yet this highly critical role is often considered the backroom work that the staff developer does to actually implement professional learning experiences. Whether it be a small-group gathering for a book study, an opening day initiative for one faculty, or a district level summer academy, the designer role demands attention to the planning phase of the professional development. This includes planning before, during, and after the actual professional development experience that will be orchestrated.

The design of the training is what makes or breaks the effectiveness of the training.

There is an interesting dichotomy that occurs in the designer role. In a way, it embodies the best of two worlds. One is the world of the organized individual who can pull off any deed. The other is the creative role of the artist who gets to play with the ideas and form an exciting learning experience. The designer role must call into play the organizational skills of the detail-oriented person and, at the same time, the creative aspects of the artist in designing an effective and memorable professional learning opportunity.

There is an interesting dichotomy that occurs in the designer role.

The designer role embraces the critical responsibilities of organizer—the person who taps into the managerial and administrative kinds of skills needed to execute any event. The designer role, as an organizer, demands a big-picture person who can create the appropriate context, synchronize the many elements of the project, and keep the end goal front and center while giving equal time, energy, and attention to the details of implementing each phase. This aspect of the designer/organizer role is responsible for planning for the actual facilities, essential content, and daylong logistics of the session(s).

At the same time, the designer taps into the most creative skills of the staff developer as artist, performer, and critic. The designer possesses the creative task of planning a dynamic session that simultaneously imparts key content while also inspiring participants to go on and do something with the skills and concepts that can effect needed change. This artist/designer must balance the management of materials, performances, and products with the challenge of creating an overall feeling on the part of participants of the worth and relevance of the professional learning.

In sum, the designer role may appeal to staff developers because they excel as organizers who get things done in expert ways or because they cherish the creativity involved in designing a work of art. In some cases, of course, the staff developer may covet the dual responsibilities the designer role offers. At the end of the day, both sets of abilities are critical to sound professional development design.

THREE ESSENTIAL ELEMENTS   ■

In each of the four roles of the staff developer, the magic number of three elements seems to emerge for further consideration. In the role of designer, organizer, and artist (or perhaps producer), the three actions include (1) planning, (2) providing, and (3) preparing. While each of the three actions is integral to the other, each also stands alone. In fact, the three elements have very specific tasks to be executed to accomplish the overall design.

Planning the Experience

Designer as organizer. The designer as organizer uses a multitude of planning tools that range from calendars and schedulers to site information, participant lists, and name tags. To orchestrate a training session requires the skill of the master puppeteer, pulling numerous strings at just the right moment for the desired effect. There are so many logistical details that often the best method is to create a standard checklist (Form 4.1) to avoid any oversights.

In turn, there are certain forms that seem helpful in organizing and ensuring all details are covered. Two such forms are the contact sheet and trip sheet. As depicted in Form 4.2, the contact sheet contains all the necessary contact information—from addresses, phone/fax numbers, and e-mails to audience size, content focus, dates, times, and site information. While this is often known because the training is internal to the organization, the use of these forms is still recommended as a convenient and expedient way to standardize the operations of the professional development trainings. They ensure that everyone is on board, has the same information, and that anyone can step in a take over if necessary.

The second sheet (Form 4.3) is the trip sheet (if traveling as a consultant) or the tip sheet (if executing a training session from within the

(Text continues on page 61)

Form 4.1   Professional Development Logistics Checklist

Date of Job: _____

Contract:

_____

Consultant: _____ Topic: _____

Time:

_____

1. Client Contact Information Complete _____

2. Contract Sent _____ Contract Signed _____

3. Description Sent _____ Photo Sent _____

4. Vita Sent _____ Bio Sent _____

5. Handout Sent _____ or _____

6. Books Ordered _____ Books Sent _____

7. Equipment List Sent _____

8. Travel Information Sent _____

9. Lodging Confirmed _____ Ground Transportation
   _____

10. Site Address _____

11. Trip Sheet Complete _____

12. Final Phone Call _____

Form 4.2   Contact Sheet

Date: _____   Quoted Fee $ _____

Contract Dates: _____   Agreed Fee $ _____

Book Quantity: ____@ Price ____ Total ____   Retainer Fee $ _____

Client: _____

Referral: _____

Contact:

Name: _____

Title: _____

Address: _____

_____

_____

Phone: (w) _____   (h) _____

Fax: _____   Cell: _____

E-mail: _____

Notes:

Topics/Background Information

_____

_____

_____

_____

Audience _____ Number _____

Session

☐ Keystone   Title _____   Time _____

☐ Break Out   Title _____   Time _____

☐ All-Day Workshop   Title _____   Time _____

☐ Other   Title _____   Time_____

Form 4.3   Trip/Tip Sheet

Trip Sheet _____

Date _____ Destination _____ Handout _____ Book _____

Time _____ Contract # _____

Consultant _____ Topic _____

Client _____

Address _____

Work _____ Home _____ Fax _____

E-mail _____

Airport _____

Depart _____ Arrive _____

Depart _____ Arrive _____

Ground: ____Limo ____Rental Car ____Cab ____Shuttle ____Pick-Up

Distance to Site _____

Lodging _____

Site _____

district). This trip/tip sheet is the final check that everything is in order and ready to go. Please note that while the contact sheet is often completed early in the process, the trip/tip sheet, more likely than not, requires any number of revisits as final details fall into place. It is just the nature of the process that, as the event nears, various details (flight times, arrival and pick-up person, etc.) are managed accordingly.

The contact sheet and the trip/tip sheets are often electronically managed and sometimes combined into a single planning sheet. Yet experience has proven that the contact sheet is the "first-touch piece" as the staff developer gathers the necessary information to get started. In turn, the trip/tip sheet is the "final-touch piece" to summarize all necessary data.

Designer as artist. The second aspect of the designer role, the designer as artist, also requires drawing from the many resources to produce a coherent piece that has a beginning, a middle, and an end. The creativity of the designer is front and center as the content of the workshop or professional development experience is developed. The use of forms benefits artistic planning with efficiency and effectiveness. These forms are called planning templates, and five templates provide ready tools for this designing phase: a web of ideas for consideration, a concept map for elaboration, a fishbone analysis chart for focus, a flowchart for pacing, and an action plan for implementation.

Web of Ideas for Focus

Using the graphic organizer of the web, the staff developer in the designer role brainstorms 10–15 ideas for possible professional learning opportunities development. These are topics, issues, concerns, initiatives, or programs that are on the agenda in some way, shape, or form. These items are simply listed at this point. Anything goes, as it is brainstorm time. The list will be analyzed later and through this process certain topics take on more priority and others seem less important.

Figure 4.1 depicts a completed web, listing numerous ideas under consideration for development.

Concept Map for Elaboration

Once the web of ideas is complete and a focus idea is chosen, the concept map template is used to elaborate on the targeted topic. While the web radiates ideas into the central idea listed in the circle, the concept map radiates outward as the topic is examined and elaborated in some detail. In the process of creating a concept map, the designer again brainstorms all aspects of the focus topic that come to mind, adding as much detail as possible.

In Figure 4.2, a completed concept map shows the elaboration of details about the selected professional development topic: Examining Student Work.

Fishbone Analysis for Focus: Template With Levels

The fishbone analysis graphic is a powerful template to use in the designer role. It forces a hierarchal analysis or outline of sorts that delineates

(Text continues on page 64)

Figure 4.1   Web of Professional Development Ideas

Create a graphic or a web of ideas that includes:

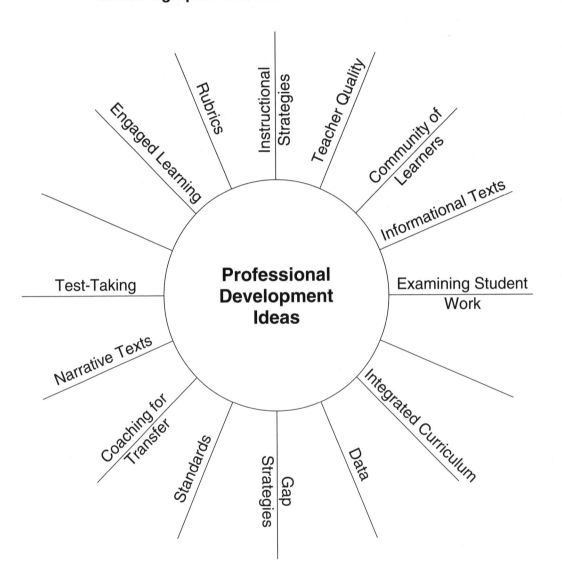

Figure 4.2   Concept Map: Examining Student Work

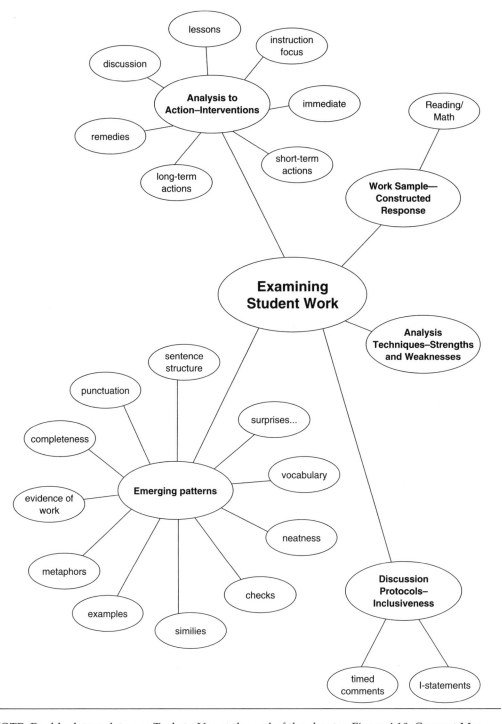

NOTE: For blank template, see Tools to Use at the end of the chapter, Figure 4.10, Concept Map.

the big idea, subtopics, and details. Much like a Harvard outline, the fishbone analysis fosters a more free-flowing analysis than the actual outline with its confining structure of Roman numerals, capital letters, numbers, and lowercase letters. Yet, the fishbone also facilitates the close examination of the entire topic under focus. Using the mapped ideas, the designer now plots the information to the fishbone model. Figure 4.3 shows the parts of the fishbone: head (target result desired), spine (theme that runs through entire training), ribs (major subheads), riblets (details that flesh out the subtopics). Figure 4.4 shows the completed fishbone as the ideas are transferred from the map to the fishbone template.

In turn, it sets up the possibility of using the "less-is-more" strategy. This strategy promotes the idea of working with one concept, one skill, or one set of skills instead of trying to do it all. This important strategy, less is more, basically calls for a dissection of many ideas into subsets that may translate into several workshops or professional development opportunities. In this second part of the exercise, the designer finds sections that are appropriate for one hour, one-half day, one day, and a summer session of multiple days. Figure 4.5 represents an example of how the designer finds various aspects of the topic for consideration.

Less is more.

One day—Protocols and Examples

One-half day—Examples to process

One hour: Example 3

Once the target content is clear, the designer is able to decide what to develop for the appropriate time slotted for the training. In essence, this is the less-is-more concept in action. Target less content and go deep with the concepts and skills rather than try to present everything at once. Adult learners prefer single concepts rather than survey courses. When there is too much content to cover, the effect is superficial. Everything stays at the surface level because there is no time to develop the piece.

While this seems to make perfect sense, it is much more difficult to do than it appears. Professional development designers often do not want to give up anything. They think all is necessary for the complete picture. Yet with practice, designers begin to understand that they can set the context, create a big-picture essence, and then focus on a particular part of the whole picture.

Flowchart for Planning, Designing, and Pacing

Now, with the focus crystallized, the actual pieces of the training puzzle come together. Following the training design of Joyce and Showers (2002) on the role of coaching, discussed at length in Chapter 7, there

(Text continues on page 68)

Figure 4.3 Fishbone Analysis: Templates With Labels

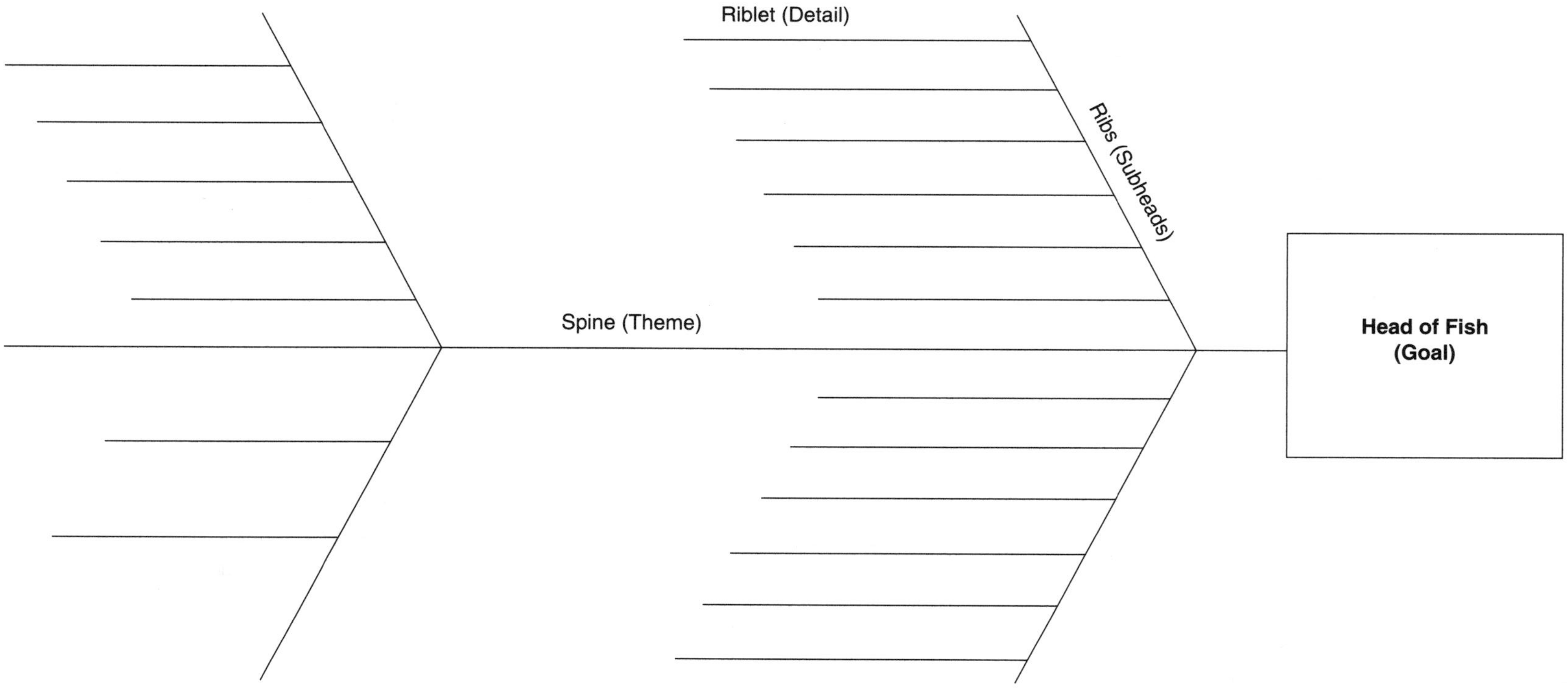

Head of Fish (Goal)

Ribs (Subheads)

Riblet (Detail)

Spine (Theme)

Figure 4.4 Completed Fishbone Analysis: Examining Student Work

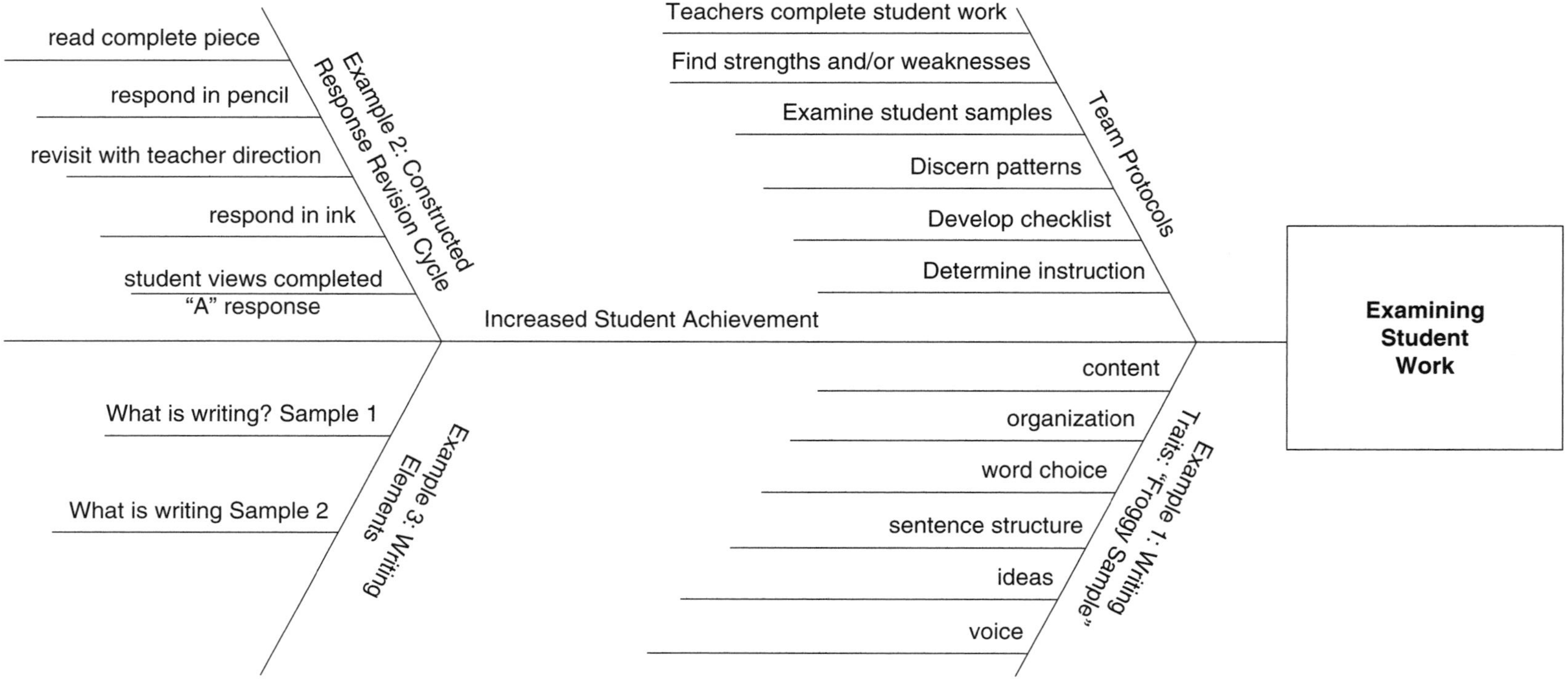

Figure 4.5 Fishbone Analysis: Less-Is-More Component

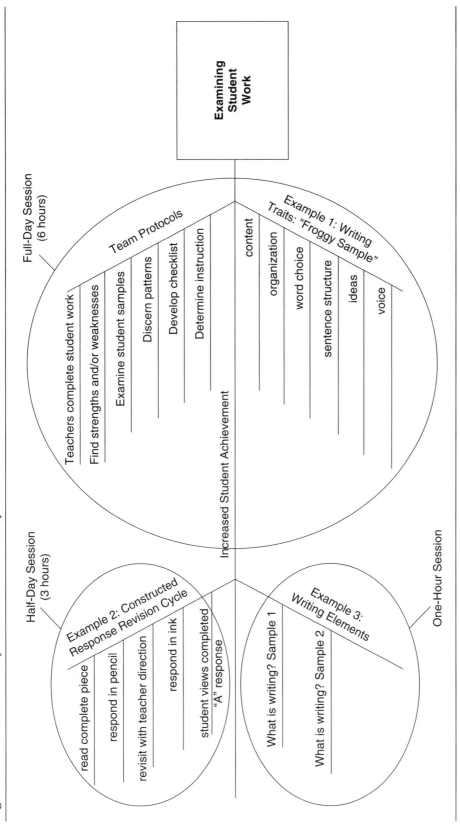

NOTE: For blank template, see Tools to Use at the end of the chapter, Figure 4.11, Fishbone Analysis.

are four elements that need to be included: (1) theory, (2) demonstration, (3) practice, and (4) coaching. These elements integrate into the overall flow of the training design using the flowchart template. This is the phase in which actual workshop or professional development opportunity begins to take shape. Figure 4.6 shows what a working flowchart plan might look like as the design unfolds. It begins with the concept, the theory, and the hook and then proceeds with input, demonstration, cooperative structure, and practice task. Finally, it ends with reflective processing, the assignment coaching plan, and closing piece.

Action Plan for Implementation

The final step in the planning phase of the design role involves a written action plan that delineates the necessary tasks to be completed, accompanied by time, dates, and details needed to make it happen. Figure 4.7 is an example. The action plan answers the questions, who needs to do what and when does it need to be done? It delineates where and how as well as the blocks and alternatives. This action plan ensures that there is a process in place for managing the complexities of tasks that spell success for the professional development plan.

Providing the Creature Comforts

Creature comforts usually revolve around two basic components: facilities and food. Proper facilities involve appropriate and comfortable settings for the adult learner. Food involves both nutritious snacks and/or meals that keep the adult brain energized and alert.

Facilities. Providing adult-sized furniture, rather than sitting in a second grade classroom with children's furniture, honors the adult learner. The appropriate setting requires tables and chairs that fit participants and facilitate their working collaboratively and independently. Although round tables are more conducive to conversation, any type of table setting is preferred to an auditorium or theater-style arrangement.

In a workshop setting, people need access to each other and the kind of comfortable furniture and environment that foster hands-on, active learning. It is in these adult learning settings that participants may truly engage in the kind of interactive learning that leads to meaningful collaborations.

Food. The most important planning considerations in this category revolve around the type, amount, and manner of the foods (breakfast, snacks, refreshments, lunch, or even dinner) that are to be served. By explicitly planning for a brain-healthy menu of items, the staff developer simultaneously accomplishes two important objectives: providing an assortment of brain-compatible foods to ensure the best possible performance from

(Text continues on page 71)

Figure 4.6 Flowchart: Examining Student Work Sample

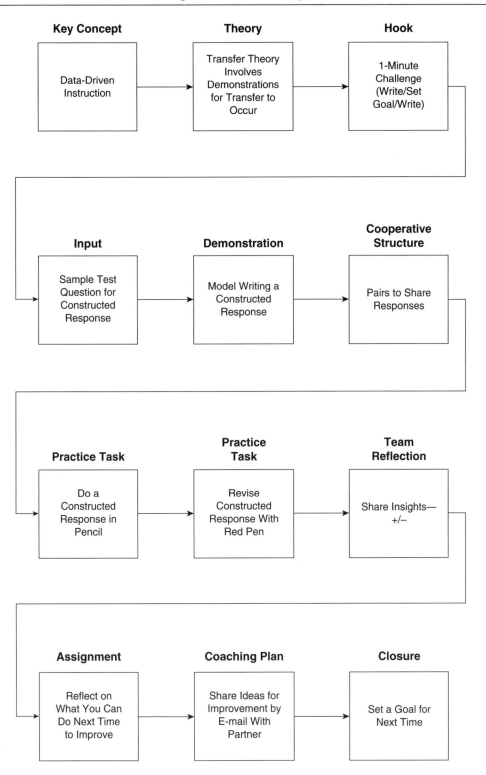

NOTE: For blank template, see Tools to Use at the end of the chapter, Figure 4.12, Flowchart.

Figure 4.7   Action Plan: Examining Student Work

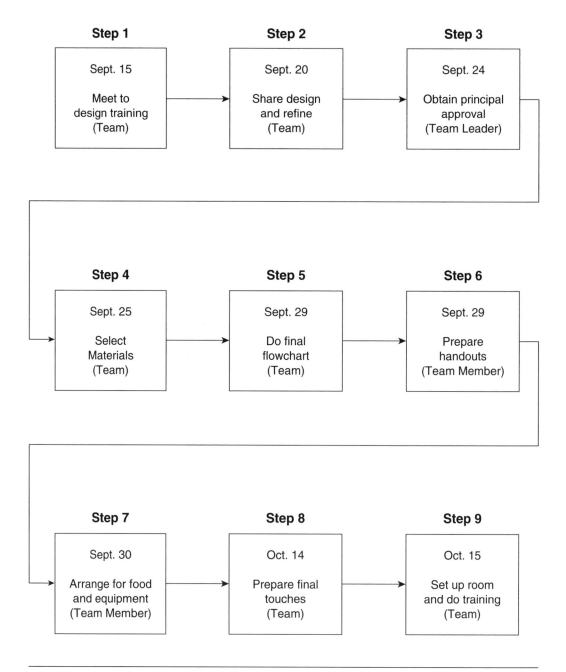

Who? What? When? Where? How? Blocks? Alternatives?

Step 1	Step 2	Step 3
Sept. 15	Sept. 20	Sept. 24
Meet to design training (Team)	Share design and refine (Team)	Obtain principal approval (Team Leader)

Step 4	Step 5	Step 6
Sept. 25	Sept. 29	Sept. 29
Select Materials (Team)	Do final flowchart (Team)	Prepare handouts (Team Member)

Step 7	Step 8	Step 9
Sept. 30	Oct. 14	Oct. 15
Arrange for food and equipment (Team Member)	Prepare final touches (Team)	Set up room and do training (Team)

NOTE: For blank template, see Tools to Use at the end of the chapter, Figure 4.13, Action Plan.

participants while modeling nutritious food selection for teachers to share and foster with their students back in the classroom.

Types. Reference the brain/heart-healthy foods in Box 4.1. Simply by cutting back on the sugars and carbohydrates and focusing on the amino acids that the brain and body obtain through protein-rich foods, a more nutritious approach to learning is established. By including foods full of omega B complex, found in fish and nuts and berries, the brain is served its best fuel.

Brain-Healthy, Heart-Healthy Foods

The following are brain-healthy/heart-healthy foods: blueberries, nuts, fish, broccoli, bananas, yogurt, olive oil, brown bread, spinach, and tomatoes. Recent news articles report on a number of items that might be added to this initial listing including several spices (cinnamon, rosemary, and thyme) some fruits and nuts (kiwis, pomegranates, walnuts), and—a surprising entry—semisweet dark chocolate (80% cocoa). Try this activity using memory pegs for brain foods by touching the designated body part.

- Blueberries—forehead
- Cinnamon—nose
- Rosemary/Sage—both eyes
- Apples—mouth
- Almonds/Walnuts—shoulders
- Salmon—chest
- Kiwis/pomegranates—sides
- Broccoli—belly button
- Bananas—hips
- Yogurt—buttocks
- Olive oil—thighs
- Whole wheat—knees
- Spinach—legs
- Tomatoes—feet
- Dark chocolate—hands up in air

Box 4.1

SOURCE: Adapted from Conyers and Wilson, 2001, BRAINSMART Nutrition: 10 Foods That May Support a Healthy Brain-Body System (www.BrainSMART.com).

Amounts. Food portions also contribute to learning effectiveness. Small servings of the right foods (high-protein foods and fruits and vegetables) leave participants nourished and energetic, while large servings of the wrong foods (mashed potatoes, gravy, dressing) leave participants feeling full and becoming more and more lethargic as the day proceeds. Having water available, limiting the availability of caffeine (coffee, tea, cokes, chocolate), and pacing meals or snacks, the staff developer, through food, creates an environment where optimal learning may occur.

Manners. Plan a vigorous activity following the meal or snack in which participants are moving about rather than sitting passively. The movement component is as important as the proper foods. It's simple brain science: The brain needs oxygen, so movement facilitates the process of oxygenating the brain. A learning environment that feeds the brain, not just with knowledge but with oxygen through moving about, contributes to effective professional development.

Plan a vigorous activity following the meal or snack.

Benefits. Interestingly, once people are served nutritious snacks, they are appreciative and complimentary about what the staff developer has provided. They sometimes note how much more alert and energetic they feel. In turn, they begin to become more conscious of the foods and their impact on learning. Often they start to rethink the impact of what the kids in their own classrooms are eating, so the focus on nutrition during professional development, while subtle, is dramatic in its effect.

Preparing the Actual Setting

Successfully accomplishing the third element of the designer role, providing creature comforts, requires the staff developer to turn to those basic human needs that can make or break a training day. Among these is room and set-up, technical equipment, materials, and supplies. If participants are too cold or hot, can't see the screen or hear the speaker, if they are missing a handout or the book, nothing else matters to them. Like a pebble in a shoe, these minor annoyances will be all that the participants will think about. That's what's on their "screen." Thus it is worthwhile, if possible, to take the time to do a site visit to ensure that all of the physical conditions are right. If not possible, clear communication with hotel staff about these issues prior to training will have to do.

Room arrangement. The room arrangement must reflect the kinds of teaching/learning processes that will occur. The designer is responsible for checking seating arrangements. It is a well-known secret that part of the job of the staff developer is moving furniture. Figure 4.8 depicts the basic design preferred by many staff developers. It angles the tables so participants may see the trainer and screen and see and talk easily to each other as they work in table teams. Last, knowing that the brain can only embrace what the bottom can endure, the designer arranges for a room with comfortable chairs.

> *The room arrangement must reflect the kinds of teaching/learning processes that will occur.*

Figure 4.8   Seating Arrangement

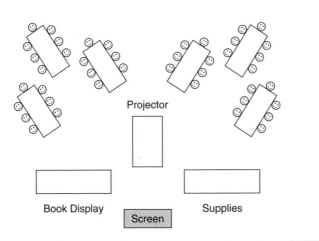

Projector

Book Display   Screen   Supplies

In addition, the staff developer must check the lighting with the blinds closed and with them open. Seating arrangements should allow visual clarity for everyone, no matter where seated, and that no one's vision is hampered by the sun or blocked by equipment. The staff developer must also know how to control the temperature in the room, if possible. It is often wise to suggest participants wear layered clothing to ensure their own comfort level.

Equipment. The staff developer must check out how to operate the audio or visual equipment. Try out and adjust the sound levels, size, contrast, and focus of the images on the screen.

> *The designer in this phase of the role must become a bit of a technician.*

The designer in this phase of the role must become a bit of a technician. A brief discussion of the various A/V equipment requirements and possible concerns follows in greater detail.

Supplies. The staff developer must order and sometimes carry these supplies to the workshop site. In Box 4.3 is a typical list of materials, including thin and fat markers, copy paper, large poster paper, sticky notes, and index cards.

Equipment List

Data Projectors for Presentation Software

- Order large screen.
- Order power strip and extension cord. Secure flat to floor with duct tape.
- Check input from computer to projector for large display.
- Check remote access.
- Check lights and use dimmer near screen if possible.
- On your computer, hit the "b" key for a black screen, "w" for white screen.

Overhead Projectors and Screen

- Check projection to screen for large display.
- Check for visibility from all seats.
- Clean glass if needed.
- Check for spare bulbs and how to switch.
- Face audience (if right handed, set up on left side and vice versa).

Videos, VCRs, and DVDs

- Use VCR if you order it.
- Cue up video and test the VCR.
- Large group, order a video projection with large screen.
- Show 8–10 minute segments with an assigned task during viewing.
- Use DVD with sound system.
- Cue appropriate chapter ahead of time.
- Limit time to 5–8 minutes.

Microphones

- Request mike for more than 40 people.
- Lavaliere or cordless lapel mike.
- Request cordless mike for audience responses if you want that.
- Check sound before audience gets there.
- Change the batteries at lunch time.
- Have backup batteries at all times.

Supplies List

Materials

Flip chart

Flip chart paper (4 sheets per table)

Large "fat" markers (4 per table)

Copy paper, 2 reams (white/color)

Fine "skinny" markers (1 per participant)

Room Arrangement

Long table in front

Table on side for book display

Supply table on other side

2 small bottles of water

Box 4.3

Materials. Last, but not least, the designer role of the staff development job takes responsibility for ordering and arranging for the delivery of books and/or duplicating the handouts or articles for the session. Some prefer full-page copies while others create three or six slides to the page from the electronic slide show. Now, more often than not, the handouts are created and sent electronically for duplication. This facilitates speedy delivery and a clear copy that satisfies the client.

Materials and Supplies

Flip Charts

- Use fat markers.
- Alternate colors for every other line.
- Outline key points.
- Put a "brain-friendly" border on page to "chunk" the information visually for the viewer.

Box 4.4 (Continued)

Supplies

- Order name tags for each day.
- Order newsprint or chart paper (2 sheets per 4 people).
- Order big watercolor markers (4 per table).
- Order sticky notes (3×3 square, 1 per table).
- Order 10 blank transparencies and 4 pens.
- Order ream of copy paper for journals, notes, etc.

Books or Handouts

- Use books or booklets whenever possible to support training with professional resources.
- Order books in advance and request confirmation.
- For one-day awareness, select 10–15 pages and create the handout—the client to duplicate.
- Number the pages for easy reference.
- Keep a copy in your folder so you know what you sent.

Transparencies/Slides

- Make transparencies or slides from the handout or book pages or design with presentation software.
- Use color to emphasize.
- Organize transparencies/slides by number or by folders in sequence.

Form 4.4   Designer Role Rubric: To Be Completed by Reader

	Developing	Competent	Proficient	Exceptional
Planning the Experience	(Sketchy)	(Plug and Play)	(Appropriate)	(Customized)
Providing the Creature Comforts	(No Snacks)	(Traditional Sweets)	(Healthy Choices)	(Protein Rich)
Preparing the Actual Setting	(Auditorium)	(Cafeteria)	(Classroom)	(Library)

■ TOOLS TO USE

1. Professional Development Conceptual Focus: Web

Figure 4.9   Web of Ideas Blank Template

Create a graphic or a web of ideas

2. Professional Development Conceptual Focus: Concept Map

Figure 4.10   Concept Map Blank Template

Show a concept map graphic depicting:

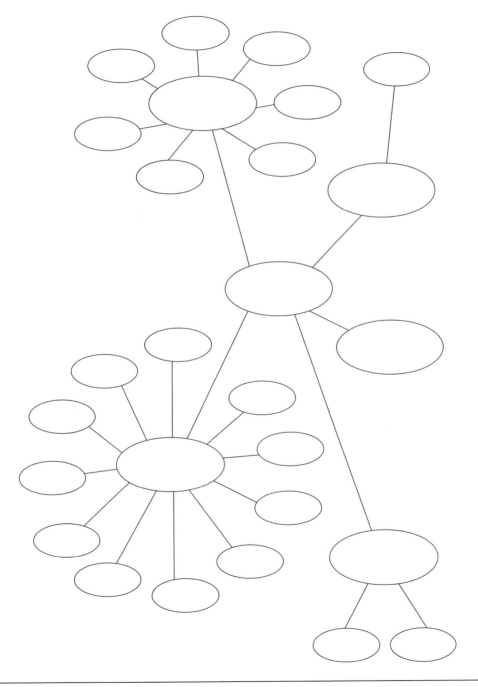

3. Fishbone Analysis: Less Is More

Figure 4.11 Fishbone Analysis Blank Template

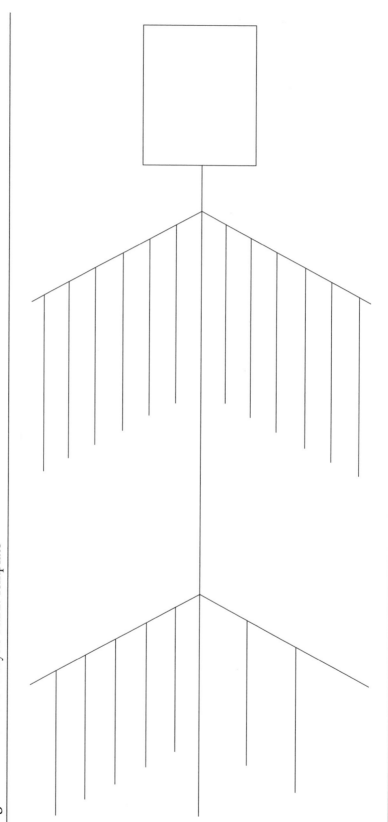

4. Flowchart for Planning, Designing, and Pacing

Figure 4.12   Flowchart Blank Template

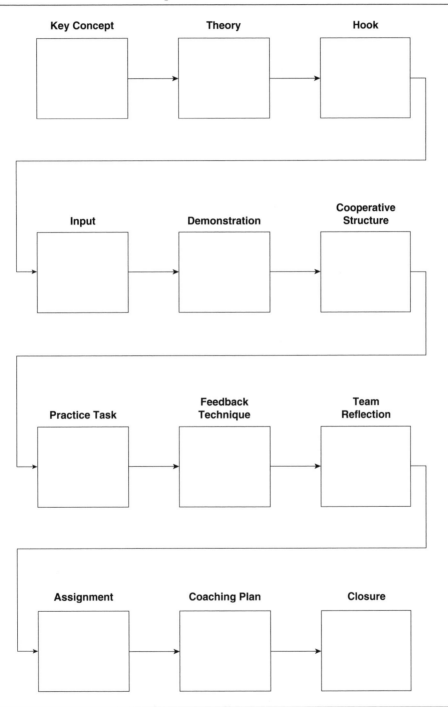

5. Putting it Together/Action Steps

Figure 4.13   Action Plan Blank Template

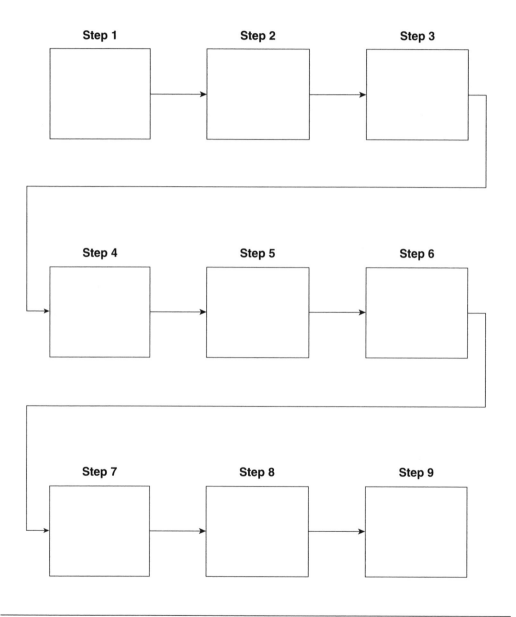

Who? What? When? Where? How? Blocks? Alternatives?

6. T-Chart Activity

Read the synopsis in Box 4.5 and create a T-chart (Figure 4.14) to operationalize the role of designer at the site. Tell specifically what it looks and sounds like when the staff developer is in the role of designer at the site.

Designer Role

Plan the workshop context, content, and concepts for customized programs tailored to the needs of the group.

Provide for the creature comforts that make or break the workshop.

Prepare the site for an optimal learning experience that supports adult learning theory and best practices.

Box 4.5

Figure 4.14   Designer Role: T-Chart

Looks Like	Sounds Like
Specifically what the staff developer does	Specifically what the staff developer says

5

A Guide to the Role of Presenting Professional Learning Experiences

Vignette: Walk the Talk; Model the Model

The symbolic story told by one seasoned staff developer speaks to the concept of the presenter as one who walks the talk, rather than talks the talk. It involves a conference session with six learning styles experts. During an evening presentation in which these invited learning styles gurus presented their work to an eagerly waiting audience, not one of them varied the presentation technique from a one-way verbal broadcast.

One after another, these experts—these researchers, writers, and consultants on learning styles—talked on and on about their ideas, never once detouring from the spoken path. Not one member of the panel incorporated even the slightest hint of learning style techniques other than that of stand and deliver. Ironically, there was not a single example or a shred of evidence of the learning styles repertories these leaders were advocating for teachers to use in their presentations.

The obvious point of the story is that if speaking about humor, one must model being humorous; if presenting on teaching and learning pedagogy, one must use best practice and sound pedagogy; if talking about a rainbow of learning styles, one must show at least some of the colors of that rainbow.

THE PRESENTING ROLE   ■

Description of the Role

The presenter role is one of the most obvious—and often one of the most visible—roles of the staff developer. It is, in essence, the role of "sage on the stage." This is the time, in staff development sessions, for the one-way broadcast. It is the point in professional learning experiences when the presentation of information is made; the input is shared and the expert gets to exhibit his wizardry on the audience. In this role, the presenter is seen as the content expert, the go-to person on the topic. In an attempt to communicate the critical concepts, key skills, and important information, the effective presenter often exhibits a wide range of abilities, including storytelling, acting, stand-up comedy, and classic oration.

> *The expert gets to exhibit his wizardry on the audience.*

While the role of designer seems more inward, the role of presenter is definitely more outward. The presenter has a clear and cunning mission to get the message out to the audience. This role requires the staff developer to instantly become a people person, a salesman of sorts, extolling his message to all who will listen and attempting to rally those who will not. The memorable presenter knows the skills of the trade. He knows how to open and get the audience on his side, how to keep the group's undivided attention, and how to end with an unforgettable finish.

Sage on the Stage: Presenting the Information

Some love this part of staff development. These are the naturally outgoing people who love to ham it up. The role of presenter provides the perfect opportunity for this extroverted talent to show itself. Thus, the presenter role is a role that is cherished by many who enjoy facing the challenge of great communication.

> *The presenter role is a role that is cherished by many who enjoy facing the challenge of great communication.*

In fact, it is often this high-profile role of staff development that brings a person into the field in the first place. It is a key component in the complex fabric of staff development, and all who enter into this field of academia must strive for great skillfulness in the presenter's role. They must work hard at becoming the best they can be in this front-and-center-stage position, even if it is not their favorite job responsibility. The staff developer who puts on the presenter's hat must truly work the magic of compelling theater.

The elusive elements involved in presentation range from the enigmatic element called "stage presence" to voice quality, sense of humor, charisma, and ability to connect with and read an audience. There is an obvious abundance of materials on how to make a good presentation, running the gamut from articles and books to courses, training films, and online videos. Although the skills of presenting are very teachable, at the end of the day, there is a particular quality—at one time called "sparkle"— that functions as the secret ingredient for presenters who are admired, emulated, and often envied.

Three Essential Elements

Staff developer responsibilities of the presenter involve three essential responsibilities: (1) *capture* the attention of the audience; (2) keep them *attentive, captivated,* and interested; and (3) *close the session* with a recap of important points. The presenter role requires a charismatic personality, skillful communicative maneuvers, and effective measures to ensure memorable closures. In short, the presenter captures the group's interest, moves group members along with captivating oratory, and closes with efficiency and purpose.

Capturing With Personality

There are three critical components of this stage of the presentation. Just as presenters must capture the attention and sensitivities of the audience, they must also include three specific elements at the very beginning of their presentation: a formal introduction, a sparkling opening segment, and an opportunity or method for displaying an agenda.

Introduction. Staff developers, in the role of presenters, must have a formal introduction. It is a rule of law! The introduction by an authority figure in charge, or even by a trusted colleague, is a necessary element to set the bar for the day. The audience wants to know the who, what, and why of the training. They need to hear a litany of credentials that positions this presenter as an expert whom they will want to hear. They want to know what's in store for them, and they want to get a feel for their expert.

> *Staff developers, in the role of presenters, must have a formal introduction. It is a rule of law!*

Skillful presenters have a biographical sketch ready for the person to use as they prepare for the introduction. When asked if they want to be introduced, they say an emphatic, "Yes, that would be wonderful!" If someone says, and they sometimes do, "I'll let you tell them about yourself," the experienced presenter explicitly requests a brief intro-duction. One might say, "I'd prefer a word from you about my work. You can just tell them . . . blah, blah, blah, if you wouldn't mind?"

In sum, the introduction is not an option. It is a crucial part of setting the stage for a successful day. The introduction is a presentation of the expert's calling card to the audience as a whole. It often includes three areas of information: (1) facts and accomplishments, (2) expertise and pas-sions, and (3) interests and personality traits. It is a proper and powerful piece of the opening ceremonies, no matter how small or how grand.

As a postscript, the introduction should be the final statement from the organizer or convener. All the logistical care-and-comfort items should be given prior to the introduction of the key speaker.

Opener. The *opener* is what the presenter does or says at the opening moment of the presentation. It is the first "bit" of the day. This is the moment when the presenter wins over the audience with bril-liance and grace. There is an old wives' tale that a presenter coming on stage has 90 seconds to make a good first impression. Skillful presen-ters know the tricks of the trade: leading with a personal insider's comment about the group or telling a joke with the perfect tenor and timing for the audience at hand. Skillful presenters hit their stride the moment they open their mouths. They know whom they are talking to and the message their audience needs and wants to hear.

> *There is an old wives' tale that a presenter coming on stage has 90 seconds to make a good first impression.*

Presenters of this level and stature are seasoned performers, and they have their openings down pat. They know the weight that opening remarks carry and have an arsenal of practiced and proven patterns of patter that work every time. These presenters know only too well that the sooner they get the audience in sync with them, the easier things are going to go and the smoother the session will be.

Agenda. Once they have that opening piece skillfully in place, presenters welcome their audience, set expectations for them, and try to procure some immediate information about them. As part of the introductory segments, presenters often do a quick survey of the audience: elementary, middle, or high school teachers? Grade level, departments represented? Number of years of experience? Who has had previous training with the topic?

Presenters know they must then project a brief agenda, a road map, previewing what's to come. Some simply tell a little about the events of the day, in broad brush stokes; others present a written agenda on the screen; or others may write the key points on a chart. Whatever the selected method, a glimpse at the big picture is needed.

Captivating With Skill

Once the presenter has captured the audience's attention, how does the presenter keep the audience with him throughout the presentation? What are the elements of an effective presentation? What are the qualities that engage an audience? Naturally, the answers to these questions are somewhat elusive, yet there are some common threads that emerge.

In the repertoire of skillful presenters there is quite a variety of tactics: stories, visuals, facts, data and information, humor, movement, and interactions.

Stories. Everyone loves a story. As soon as someone says, "I want to tell you a story," ears perk up and the audience is poised to listen. Stories embed larger messages in such endearing ways that the lesson itself may be soon forgotten while the story lingers and remains with the audience. Good presenters find the stories that illustrate their key points and sprinkle them throughout their presentation to punctuate their message.

A picture is worth a thousand words.

Visuals. "A picture is worth a thousand words." Using visuals adds a powerful dimension to any presentation. After all, 80 percent of all input to the brain is visual. It is the visual that often stays in the mind long after the actual presentation is complete.

The visual may be any of the following: demonstrations and modeling; overhead transparencies; electronic presentations; authentic artifacts; prototypes or samples; or video, film, or DVD clips. The visual may be pictures, charts, cartoons, drawings, and samples of student or teacher work.

Facts, data, and information. Nothing is more compelling than facts, data, and information to support the message. They must be presented, however, in a format that is highly visible, easily readable, and in small enough doses to digest readily. Using clear charts, graphs, and tables that are color coded, large, and distinct enough from each other can give the audience compelling, succinct, and credible information. All presenters will definitely use the facts and data they have, but skillful presenters will use them with care and clarity.

Humor. There is nothing as effective as the joke, riddle, or quip, timed perfectly and used to make a telling point or summarize a big idea. Humor is the great deflector! It gives the mind a moment to rest, and it relaxes the tension of a PowerPoint presentation. Presenters who have a record of quality presentations also have a warehouse of humorous tales to tell.

Movement. Movement is another visual that helps captivate the attention of the audience. Just by moving from one position to another on the stage, moving vertically up or down, or standing and then crouching down to the audience, presenters can keep the eyes of the audience on them. It's that little bit of movement that attracts and holds attention.

Interactions. Finally, a bit of movement for the audience is always appropriate. Having them stand or raise their hands or turn to a partner to respond to an idea are skillful tactics to keep the audience cued and alert.

Read the audience. A good presentation stems from the ability to read the audience. The presenter who knows when to shift the focus, change the pace, or get the group moving and interacting is the well-prepared presenter. Perhaps the most common fatal flaw in a new or inexperienced presenter is this inability to read the audience and shift gears immediately. While they know their content backward, forward, and upside down, the skillful presenter also knows it's all about the audience. They come first and must be tuned in or the presentation goes nowhere.

> *While they know their content backward, forward, and upside down, the skillful presenter also knows it's all about the audience.*

Closing With "Keepers"

The close is as important as the opening. It is what the learners take away: What is the message in a bottle? What is the recap? What are the key phases, telling points, summations? What is the quote? What is the one thing to leave with, if nothing else?

Here are a few pointers for a solid and effective close to the presentation. Some are tips of the trade that are essential, required for success; others are optional.

Required:

1. End early, never late. The payoff is worth it.
2. Revisit the big picture with a story or quote. Leave them thinking.
3. Validate the worth of the content. Connect the relevance.
4. Summarize key points with a visual. There's that picture again.
5. Acknowledge the audience. Congratulate them on their cooperation and contributions.
6. Use a specific closing activity. Go for it!
7. Push for transfer. Encourage and energize the group to take action.

Optional:

8. Distribute evaluation forms, if appropriate.
9. Give door prizes, if appropriate.

Closure activities. 3-2-1 Connect and Reflect. Ask participants to think about and share in three separate interactions as they move from one person to the next:

3 recalls

2 insights

1 question

Yellow Brick Road. Ask participants to go to one corner of the room that best describes where they are in terms of the topic under study. Instruct them to discuss their reflections with others in their group.

Corner 1: Under Construction

Corner 2: Rocky Road

Corner 3: Yellow Brick Road

Corner 4: Highway to Heaven

and . . . Middle of Room: Dirt Path

4-1-1 Dial Information. Ask participants to think about and share with a partner:

4 new facts or ideas

1 thing they knew already

1 call to action

■ TOOLS TO USE

1. First Impressions

Using the following lead-ins, write about the most memorable presenter in your experiences.

1. Name someone you believe is a great presenter.
2. Tell two traits of your presenter.
3. Describe someone who is not a great presenter.
4. Tell how the two are significantly different.
5. Write a concluding sentence.

2. Skillful Presentations

Rank the following according to your strengths and weaknesses.

_____ Present the big picture.

_____ Stay on task and follow the agenda.

_____ Vary the pace.

_____ Connect ideas.

_____ Flex with the circumstance (shorten/lengthen).

_____ Foster reflection.

_____ Encourage questions and interaction.

_____ Check for understanding.

Presenter Role Rubric

Form 5.1   Presenter Role Rubric (to be completed by reader)

	Developing	Competent	Proficient	Exceptional
Capturing With Personality	(Momentary)	(Memorable)	(Compelling)	(Unforgettable)
Captivating With Skill	(Attentive)	(Engrossed)	(Captivated)	(Compelled)
Closing With Keepers	(Summary)	(Key Points)	("Punch Line")	("Stickiness Factor")

3. Survey and Rate

Rate the following Presenter tools on a scale of 1 to 10, with 10 as the best.

1. Visual tools

_____ Electronic Presentation (PowerPoint/Keynote)

_____ Charts

_____ Transparencies

_____ Video/Film

2. Auditory tools

_____ Music

_____ Voice quality/articulation

_____ Sound signals

3. Nonverbal tools

_____ Movement

_____ Actions (hand gestures, signals)

4. T-Chart Activity

Read the following synopsis in Box 5.1 and create a T-chart (Figure 5.1) to operationalize the role of sage on the stage. Tell specifically what it looks like and sounds like when the staff developer is in the role of presenter on the stage.

Presenter Role

Capture . . . the audience and get their focused attention for the session; tell them what you're going to do.

Captivate . . . the audience and keep them with you with expert information that enhances their understanding of the topic; do it.

Close . . . through comments that revisit and emphasize key learnings to take away; tell them what you did.

Box 5.1

Figure 5.1   Presenter Role: T-Chart

Looks Like	Sounds Like
Specifically what the staff developer says	Specifically what the staff developer says

6

A Guide to the Role of Facilitating Professional Learning

Vignette: Who's Doing the Talking?

Arriving at an urban elementary school, the reading consultant asks for a walk-through of the building to get a feel for what is going on in the K–8 classrooms. As she moves through the two-story structure, she stops by various doorways, pokes her head into some rooms, and listens and watches for a minute or two. She has the eyes and the ears of the seasoned teacher and draws much from these momentary glimpses into the day-to-day occurrences of the classroom. As the walk-through comes full circle and she finds herself back at the main office area, she sits with the principal for a quick debriefing. She sums up her impression.

She says, "The person doing the talking is the person doing the learning. The person doing the talking is the person making mindful connections in an effort to communicate those thoughts to others. The person doing the talking is constructing meaning in the mind."

> Then, she asks a compelling question of the principal: "When you walk through the building, who's doing the talking?"
>
> When the principal replies, "The teachers are doing most of the talking," the consultant says, "I think I'll begin with a workshop titled, 'Who's Doing the Talking?' In that way, I can focus teachers on balancing direct instruction and with more facilitation, getting kids more actively involved in the learning. What do you think?"

■ THE FACILITATING ROLE

Description of the Role

In contrast to the more dominating role of the presenter, or sage on the stage, in adult learning the more obscure and subtle role is that of the group facilitator. As the group facilitator, the staff developer focuses on keeping the participants participating. This is when the one-way broadcast of the presenter role shifts to the *learning* position of the participants.

I teach, but they must learn.

Embracing the slogan, "I teach, but they must learn," the facilitator skillfully maneuvers the situation so that the participants become actively involved in the teaching-learning process. This facilitator role complements the presenter role in that teaching-learning equation by inviting participants to become involved and invested in the learning process.

Using myriad strategies to engage the adult learner, skillful facilitators know the tricks of the trade. They know how to gradually move participants from interested onlookers or even passive, disengaged learners to active/interactive players who eventually take ownership for their learning. This ability to get the participants involved, or on your side, as a trainer, staff developer, or presenter is no easy task. It takes knowledge, skill, personality, and patience to find the appropriate tools and proper tenor to accomplish this.

Some of the most effective tools for facilitators in getting the participant into the actual learning side of the equation include engaging independent activities, collaborative models, cooperative learning structures, and multimodal learning with a multiple-intelligences approach.

Engaging, independent activities are often hands-on tasks, such as responding to an agree/disagree chart of statements, reflecting in a journal, or responding to a learning log lead-in statement. Collaborative learning models range from simple "Meet and Greet Your Tablemates" to "Turn to Your Partner, and . . ." (TTYPA) to find two others you don't know and form a "Three Musketeers Team."

Cooperative learning includes small-group structures (Kagan, 1989): Think, Pair, Shares, A Pair of Pairs, Four Heads Together, and Tear/Share Foursome. It also includes whole-group activities such as the Human Graph and the People Search. In addition to these interactive strategies, the multiple-intelligences approach fosters authentic involvement using the various intelligences (Gardner, 1983), for example, visual intelligence in drawing, sketching, and illustrating or the bodily kinesthetic intelligence used in creating a role-play or a dance.

Guide on the Side: Facilitating the Process

In brief, the role of the facilitator takes the focus off the presenter and the input stage and puts it firmly on the learner and the output stage. Facilitation is about guiding the learning process—from the sidelines. The effective facilitator designs the interaction, sets it up, and makes sure everyone is on board. She monitors the work, intervening as necessary to keep the learning for each individual or each team at the highest level possible.

It is truly a gift for the staff developer to learn the skills of group facilitation, for this is where the rubber hits the road, so to speak. Facilitation answers the questions, "Can the participants internalize the key concepts and skills that have been presented, and can they demonstrate their understanding in authentic ways?"

> It is truly a gift for the staff developer to learn the skills of group facilitation.

Three Essential Elements

There are three essential elements of skillful facilitation, including the ability to *invite* participants to join in the learning activities, *involve* them intensely so they become engaged, and foster their *interpretation* of what is what and how they work as a group. These three I's—invite, involve, interpret—demand further explanation and are more fully discussed in the following sections.

Inviting . . . Collegiality

The shift from the role of sage on the stage to the complementary role of guide on the side is epitomized in the invitation to participants to fully take part in group interactions. Some of these interactions are informal and quick; others require explicit structure and instructions from the facilitator.

Informal

Informal interactions are woven into the workshop so participants feel comfortable working with each other. These informal activities model the act of meeting a new group or introducing oneself to someone. These are life skills that one encounters everywhere, so the opportunity to practice these kinds of interpersonal skills is time well spent. Within the realm of informal interactions are the following: Meet and Greet, Turn to Your Partner and . . . , Invite a Stranger to Lunch, Change Groups, Find a New Partner.

Meet and Greet

As a first interaction, the facilitator may simply say, "Meet and greet your tablemates," as a quick, yet deliberate way to be sure all members of the table team know each other's names. It takes just a moment, but it totally changes the tenor of the room from stiff and separate to relaxed and collaborative.

Turn to Your Partner and . . . (TTYPA . . .)

Almost everyone has experienced the clear and direct announcement from the facilitator to "Turn to your partner and talk about this idea." This may seem like a spontaneous moment, yet, truth be known, the facilitator slots these brief interactions to create the appropriate amount of engagement and pacing in the session. It offers a needed breather for participants. It gives them a chance to make sense of the information in personal ways as they communicate with each other.

Three Musketeers

Discovered in a session with Kagan (1989), this wonderful interaction quickly motivates participants to move about and find two new partners. The facilitator says, "Put your hand up and find two others with their hands up to form a teepee with your hands." Once they are together as a three musketeers group, the facilitator structures the interaction, "Find three things you all like, three things you all hate, and something unique about each of you, and . . . share with your teammates."

Invite a Stranger

One of the best little strategies for integrating the members of a group is when the facilitator says, "Invite a stranger or a strange one to lunch with you or your group. Meet as many new colleagues today as you can."

Changing Groups

Invite a stranger or a strange one to lunch with you or your group.

Facilitators often ask participants to find a new group. It is a sure way to expose the more extroverted members as they willingly move to a new table or team. It is also a cue to those who may need more prodding to meet new people.

New Partners

Finding new partners is similar to moving into new groups. Some are very comfortable with this while others need a little help to actually find that new person. And still others will never change, no matter what skills the facilitator employs. These reluctant ones somehow find ways to stay put and avoid the social risk of being rejected. If they just sit by, however, someone usually goes over to them.

Formal

To use cooperative structures successfully, there are several decisions to make in forming groups for interactivity. These decisions include the following elements: task, size, makeup, roles, product, assessment, and reflection, as reflected in the Form 6.1.

(Text continues on page 99)

Form 6.1   Decisions for Forming Cooperative Learning Groups

Task: What is the assignment?

Size: How many?

Make Up or Composition: Who? Why?

Roles: Responsibilities needed?

(Continued)

Form 6.1 (Continued)

Product: Outcomes expected?

Assessment: How evaluated?

Reflection: How to look back?

Task

The task becomes the pivot point for many of the other decisions. Once the facilitator determines what participants will do, the size of the teams, their composition, and roles become clear. For example if a team must do a complex task such as creating a three-dimensional model, they may need the role of a "traveler" to scout out other ideas.

Size

Pairs or partners work well in many situations; threes are always appropriate according to Johnson, Johnson, and Holubec (1986, 1988). Kagan (1989) prefers fours as the basic group size because the facilitator has flexibility to use the foursome as a pair of pairs or use the pairs as partners.

Makeup or Composition

Heterogeneous or homogeneous? The research suggests that heterogeneous or mixed-ability groupings are best. Johnson and colleagues (1986, 1988) say, "The more diverse the group, the richer the product." Yet there may be a few times when a homogeneous group is more appropriate, for example, when participants are placed in job-alike groups for a particular task or when participants select a group based on abilities, talents, or interests.

> *The more diverse the group, the richer the product.*

Roles

The roles assigned to groups are determined by the task at hand, and these are depicted in Box 6.1. Yet, there are several roles that have become almost generic in nature because they are useful in many situations. These include the following:

- Materials manager—Gets the stuff
- Recorder—Records the notes and ideas
- Reporter—Speaker for the group
- Encourager—Cheerleader for the group
- Traveler—Scouts out ideas

Roles and Responsibilities

• Materials manager	• Task leader
• Recorder	• Timekeeper
• Reporter	• Observer
• Encourager	• Clarifier
• Traveler	• Illustrator

Box 6.1

Other times, roles are explicitly labeled for the particular content task. To illustrate this idea, a writing task may require the roles of a scribe, editor, publisher, and distributor. A science-oriented task may have an inventor, researcher, lab technician, and spokesperson.

Product

The product may be a report or a presentation determined by the facilitator or derived by the group based on creativity, talent, skill, and interests.

Assessment

The facilitator may use traditional quizzes and tests for checking for understanding or a portfolio, product, or performance that is accompanied by a scoring rubric.

Reflection

Looking back over the interaction provides an opportunity to assess the behavior of the team and achieved outcomes. The reflection is often prompted with a lead-in question such as, "What did your team do well?" and "What might you do differently?" These reflective prompts are discussed more fully in the coaching section.

Involving . . . Authentically

The facilitator possesses a treasure chest of tactics that structure interactions in highly manageable ways and ensure full participation. Whole-group, small-group, and individual tasks make up the arsenal of tactics available to the motivated facilitator. Each type of interaction is used intentionally with a specific purpose in mind.

Whole-Group Interactions

Involving the whole group (see Box 6.2) is often a first goal of the facilitator. These interactions tend to get everyone involved at some level. They provide a way of setting a cooperative climate in the room as participants become a little more comfortable with the situation. Among the whole-group interactions are five proven strategies that get participants either peripherally involved or literally on their feet and moving about. The five whole-group interactions include Rhetorical Questions, Woven Questions, The Human Graph, The People Search, and The 2-4-8 Focus Interview. Following are explanations for each of them.

Rhetorical Questions: The facilitator asks provocative questions for the audience or participants to think about but not to actually respond to in the session. For example, "Can you imagine what that might have been like?"

Woven Questions: The facilitator weaves strategically worded questions into the lecture and targets a student for a response. For instance, "Joseph, what do you think about this theory? Does it sound feasible?"

Whole-Group Interactions

Do . . .

Rhetorical Questions

Woven Questions

Human Graph

People Search

2-4-8 Focus Interview

Box 6.2

Human Graph: A human graph is formed as the teacher asks students or participants to select a position along an imaginary axis. As each participant finds a spot, a bar graph takes shape. Participants are then encouraged to share the rationale for their position with others nearby. The graph may be formed around differing concepts such as fractions and decimals. Participants choose based on the statement: Which would you rather be, a fraction or a decimal? Or participants select their strength as a staff developer by standing on one of the four points on the fictitious graph: "Designer, Presenter, Facilitator, Mediator." See Figure 6.1.

Figure 6.1   Human Graph: Where Is Your Strength?

| Designer | Presenter | Facilitator | Mediator |

People Search: The People Search requires participants to move about the room and "Find someone who. . . ." The various "people to find" are part of a search for information around a particular subject. For example:
Topic: Change
Directions: Find someone who . . .

1. Shares a story about something she or he changed recently.

2. Compares the concept of "changing careers" to "changing channels on the TV."

. . . and so forth.

Usually there are 5–10 statements for participants to experience. Following the interaction, the presenter debriefs the group about the targeted statement to make key points.

2–4-8 Focus Interview: Two, Four, Eight Focus Interview begins with a pair, moves to a pair of pairs, and finally ends with two sets of four, or eight. This interaction works best when the participants have something in their hands to talk about, such as a book, report, item, or artifact of their work. To begin, partners share their items. Then they find another pair and share what their first partner told them. In the retelling sequence, by the time they are in the final eight, each person has told his story, his partner's story, and a third story from the foursome. It's a powerful speaking/ listening cycle for adult learners and students.

Small-Group Interactions

Small-group interactions (Box 6.3) serve to divide the large group into manageably sized segments of two to four to facilitate more frequent and intense personal interactions. The effectiveness of these activities is in the numbers. A small team gets everyone more airtime, and the small-group work is structured to do precisely that. Everyone takes part, resulting in buy-in and ownership of the task. Among the small-group interactions are included models for two or more members of the team. They include, TTYPA, Think/Pair/Share, Dyads, Trios, and Quads.

Small-Group Interactions

Do . . . TTYPA . . . (Turn to Your Partner and . . .)

Do . . . Think/Pair/Share

Do . . . Dyads—2 heads better than one

Do . . . Trios—observer role

Do . . . Quads—pair of pairs

Box 6.3

1. *TTYPA:* Turn to Your Partner and . . . connects personally with the information coming into their minds as the speaker pauses for a moment of reflection.

2. *Think/Pair/Share:* Think/Pair/Share, on the other hand, is a more formal interaction of two people than the TTYPA. In this interaction, partners first think individually about an idea. Then, two pair up and try to come to a consensus about the topic. Finally, they tell their shared ideas to others. Think/Pair/Share is an interaction of great stature in situations that must truly foster collaborations.

3. Dyads: The concept, "two heads are better than one," has been proven over and over again, in collaborative situations. The spirit of cooperation calls for a true coming together of two minds. The outcome is often far richer than when one tries to figure things out alone. The "power of two" is a well-known truth for those who work in cooperative classrooms and collaborative staff rooms. Teams of two have reflective

> *The concept, "two heads are better than one," has been proven over and over again.*

dialogues that yield much in return. Whenever possible, facilitating pairs, partners, duos, or dyads is the preferred interaction with both adults and younger students.

4. Trios: Triads offer another dimension that also often empowers a group. Trios can be as powerful as partners. In fact, the addition of that third person often gives an extra point of view that is new and unique. In addition, a third person may also be used to conduct a structured interaction of a pair, with the third party taking on the role of observer to the interaction. This is a different way of observing a behavior being practiced by the teams of two.

5. Quads: The concept of a "pair of pairs" is attributed to Kagan, who seems to prefer the method of setting up the pairs so that they may easily be grouped into fours. It works! So, it's worth a try in staff interactions, as well as those in the classroom.

Individual Endeavors

Individual endeavors are part and parcel of the facilitator's bag of tricks (Box 6.4). There comes a time in the interactive learning segments when the learner must take full responsibility for the activities that occur as part of the group's work. At this moment, participants might produce an independent project, respond to a reflective comment, or devise an action plan of sorts as evidence of learning. Sometimes this is also a last-ditch effort on the part of the facilitator to get each and every person involved and participating.

Participation: The individual in a group must take personal responsibility to participate and be involved both on his or her own and as part

---

Individual Endeavors

- Participation—Required personal, independent assignment
- Product—Designated paper, project, or presentation
- Reflection—Thoughts about the teamwork
- Action Plan—Applications of the information

Box 6.4

of group or team interactions. There is often some required personal, independent assignment structured into the interactions. This keeps each member accountable and invested in what is taking place at any given time.

Product: It is wise to have a designated paper, project, or presentation that the individual is solely responsible for doing. This is often in addition to the group or team product or presentation. It may take the form of a log or journal or even a portfolio of the work.

Reflection: Individual reflection is a key strategy as team members think about the teamwork and strengths and weaknesses of the group as a whole and, in particular, their role or part in the interactions. This is how the team and its members improve their performance for the next time.

Action Plan: Applying information in real and relevant ways is the goal of most professional learning opportunities. To facilitate this, an individual action plan is often required. This forces the learner to capture his or her own personal ideas to put new learned behaviors and values into action in relevant, meaningful, and purposeful ways.

Interpreting . . . Team Behavior

Interpreting the behavior and work ethics of the group again requires tools and tactics that structure reflection opportunities for participants. The interpretation phase often employs one or more of the following processing arenas: affective processing about feelings and emotions, cognitive processing about responses and answers, and metacognitive processing about reflections on the hows and whys.

Skillful facilitators know the power of interpretative processing—of reflection on the team and on the work. These "guides on the side" know that participants learn best about effective group activities—framed by skillful group interactions—when they are required to think explicitly about how their group behaved, what kind of teamwork they experienced, and how they might change some things for improvement next time they work together.

This is the true power of group work—modeling of authentic situations, as those experienced in life—and learning to work as a team, a committee, or a group. This modeling for adult learners transfers to the younger students in a classroom as participants become familiar with the various tactics and strategies used.

Affective processing. Affective processing is perhaps the most important means of assessing learning effectiveness, yet it is often left out as the facilitator yields to ever-present time constraints. How participants feel about certain activities and how they respond to various activities spells success or failure in terms of transfer to their classrooms. If they like what occurred, they may be tempted to try it with their students; on the other hand, if they feel that they were not very successful with the experience, they may be inclined to omit it from their action plan.

PMI: Three quick affective processing tools are the PMI, Mrs. Potter's Questions, and I Appreciate. Edward deBono's (1973) Plus Minus Interesting chart appeals to the members of the group to examine all sides of the activity—*what they like* (+), *what they didn't like* (−), or *may find interesting but more neutral* (I).

Mrs. Potter's Questions: Based on the thoughtful questions of a mentor teacher, the four queries force a thorough analysis of the activity or experience. Individually or in a small or large group, the following are the four questions posed:

Form 6.2   PMI

Plus	
Minus	
Interesting	

1. What were you supposed to do?
2. What did you do well?
3. What would you do differently next time?
4. Did you need any help?

I Appreciate: In an attempt to focus on the team-building aspect of group work, the "I appreciate . . ." statement asks for a positive comment about the group interactions or a particular member's behavior.

For example, "I appreciate the way Colin included the illustrations in the final paper. It really enhanced our product."

Cognitive processing. Cognitive processing is the typical reflection following an activity or interactions. This is the time when the facilitator surveys groups or various members for a myriad of answers, responses, or replies to the investigation or inquiry that has been conducted. It's a look at the content from the perspective of a number of people involved. It is a chance to share ideas and learn from each other. Included in the category of cognitive processing tactics are (1) "What? So, what? Now, what?" (2) "3-2-1 Connect and Reflect," (3) "Take-Away Window," and (4) "Tiny Transfer Book."

What? So, what? Now, what?: Using the three questions to revisit and review, the participants can quickly grasp the essence of the content studied. Each group or member who responds adds to the fabric of understanding.

3-2-1 Connect and Reflect: Guiding the reflection more specifically, the 3-2-1 asks participants to reply to each of the three prompts and then share those responses with another:

3 Recalls from the session

2 Insights gained

1 Burning question that remains

Take-Away Window: The Take-Away Window is a playful way to cue participants of the various ideas, concepts, skills, and strategies that they can take with them to their classrooms. It is merely an ongoing listing of the events that occurred throughout the session, revisited and reviewed at the close of the session. In this way, it acts as a cognitive reminder as participants debrief on the ideas on the list that are of the most interest to them.

Tiny Transfer Book: This a "foldable" that is used to capture the ideas for transfer. Created by participants in the session, the pages are labeled as the facilitator guides the development of the book. Instructions for the Tiny Transfer Book appear in Box 6.5.

Metacognitive processing. The most compelling kind of processing is the metacognitive reflection in which participants step aside and look back on themselves and the interaction. In this kind of reflection, queries are about how participants did things and why they did or did not work well. Value comes from how participants use this material, if they will use it. This level of reflection is about transfer and application of the learning in relevant ways specific to each learner. Several tactics foster metacognitive reflection: (1) Aha! Oh, No! (2) Mr. Parnes's Questions, and (3) Mrs. Pointdexter's Questions.

The most compelling kind of processing is the metacognitive reflection.

Aha! Oh, No!: Participants are required to think about one Aha! moment and one Oh, No! moment they had, producing insights that evaluate aspects of the learning against their teaching.

Directions for Tiny Transfer Book

1. Fold a sheet of paper in half the short way (a hamburger bun or a taco fold). Then fold it in half again, into four corners; and fold it in half one more time. When you open the paper it will have eight sections on it.

2. Now, fold the paper again into the hamburger bun. Keep the fold at the top and tear along the center vertical through the fold to the horizontal mark, half way down. If you did this correctly, there should be a hole in the middle of the paper that you can look through.

3. After the tear has been made, refold the paper the long way, like a hot dog bun or a burrito. The fold and the hole are on the top.

4. Hold both ends of the hot dog fold and push the ends toward the center (your hands are pushing toward each other) until all four sections touch. It looks kind of like a pinwheel.

5. Then, gently fold the pages around, and you have a little book with a cover and seven pages.

6. Put the ragged edges on the bottom, and you are ready to make a cover.

Box 6.5

Mr. Parnes's Questions: Asking several very lofty questions, Mr. Parnes (Parnes, 1975) takes learning to a new level—the metacognitive level: thinking about one's thinking and learning about one's learning. Mr. Parnes asks two questions that foster connection to prior knowledge and connection to future applications:

1. How does this connect to something you already know?

2. How might you use this in the future?

Mrs. Pointdexter's Questions: Mrs. Pointdexter asks two other questions that encourage participants to look at their problem-solving strategies and abilities to accept and overcome challenges. She asks the following questions that cause one to probe deeply for the answers.

1. Where did you get stuck?

2. How did you get unstuck?

Facilitator Role Rubric

Figure 6.2   Facilitator Role Rubric (to be completed by the reader)

	Developing	Competent	Proficient	Exceptional
Inviting Collegiality	(Open Door)	(Open Arms)	(Open Minds)	(Open Hearts)
Involving Authentically	(Interactive)	(Cooperative)	(Collegial)	(Learning Community)
Interpreting Team Behavior Purpose)	(Making Sense)	(Making Meaning)	(Making Personal Relevance)	(Sensing Inspired Purpose)

■ TOOLS TO USE

1. Cooperative Structures

Two-Minute Buzz

2. Roles and Responsibilities

Discussion Leader
Materials Manager
Recorder
Reporter
Researcher

3. Team Building

Three Musketeers

4. T-Chart Activity

Read the synopsis in Box 6.6 and create a T-chart (Figure 6.3) to operationalize the role of guide on the side. Tell specifically what it looks and sounds like when the staff developer is in the role of facilitator on the side.

Facilitator Role

Invite active participation through collaborative structures of pairs, trios, quads, as well as whole-group interactions.

Involve all participants in the interactions with skillful monitoring, interventions within the groups, and facilitating questions.

Interpret the results of the collaborations using reflective strategies, discuss how the team worked, pluses and minuses.

Box 6.6

Figure 6.3   Facilitator Role T-Chart

Looks Like	Sounds Like
Specifically what the staff developer says	Specifically what the staff developer says

7

A Guide to the Role of Coaching Professional Learning

Vignette: The Coach in Our Lives

To know the role of the coach is to know a coach in our own lives. Whether it is a voice coach, an acting coach, a riding coach, an athletic coach, or a literacy coach, the characteristics and qualities are similar. Coaching is personal, timely, observational, practical, relevant, responsive, sustained, and embedded in performance.

The voice of a riding coach illustrates the qualities that distinguish the coaching role from the facilitator. As she observes three different riders pass by her, her comments tell the story of coaching:

Rider #1: "Keep your head high; hug with your knees; a little more speed"

Rider #2: "Talk to him as you approach the obstacle; touch his neck; stay focused."

Rider #3: "Slow down the approach; back straight; see you and your horse as one."

In all coaching scenarios, the coaching is inextricably connected to the particular performance of the student, protégé, or mentee. It is the teaching role that depends on quality time together; a trusting relationship; and continual, ongoing two-way interactions that foster honest, candid, and gentle dialogue. Readers may think about who is, or has been, a coach in their lives—and when have they been in the role of coach for someone else.

THE COACHING ROLE ■

Another contrast to the facilitator role is that of the staff developer as coach. Many believe that this is the most intricate responsibility of the staff developer. Unlike the facilitator role, in which the guidance and movements of the facilitator are orchestrated overtly—in full view and with the complete cooperation of the entire group—the coach zeros in on particular situations, teams, or persons and counsels in more intimate and personal ways.

> *The coach zeros in on particular situations, teams, or persons and counsels in more intimate and personal ways.*

While this coaching may occasionally take place within the actual training day, the real power occurs in those day-to-day opportunities for coaching within the learners' work settings.

In fact, this is the job-embedded aspect of sound professional learning—the heart of the process of application and transfer. It is the key—the absolute key—to powerful, authentic applications. When someone is available to coach—when they are visible, available, and accessible; when they are able to be there in the heat of the action to counsel, to guide, encourage, and support in a myriad of meaningful ways—the influence on the learner is multiplied many times over.

Also, when that kind of moment-to-moment, personally relevant coaching is sustained over time, when the coach is on the scene for the long run, the results are phenomenal, unbelievable! The impact is beyond the expected. Just as the athletic champions in every arena depend on the expertise of coaches, quality teachers deserve and need the coaching of experts in their fields.

The insightful coach knows exactly when and where and how to step in to mediate, to bridge, and to extend the learning. The true coach knows the power of establishing relationships, engendering genuine rapport, and empowering others with knowledge and skills. The successful coach knows that the game, at this point in time, is more about the learner's emerging profile of wants and needs than about the staff developer's carefully prepared agenda.

> *The insightful coach knows exactly when and where and how to step in to mediate, to bridge, and to extend the learning.*

Interestingly, as the concept of staff development has evolved toward the more all-encompassing concept of continuous professional learning, the role of coaching is finding its well-deserved place in the complexities of the change agents' job. In fact, there are unprecedented numbers and types of coaches sprinkled throughout our school settings, their coaching roles falling into two distinct arenas: the expert coach and the peer coach.

Coach in the Field: Mediating the Learning

Expert Coaches

Expert coaching roles take on several different forms. Some are in the traditional role of teaching experts, such as one-on-one mentors for beginning teachers; some are content experts, such as literacy and math coaches or inclusion coaches, available to an entire staff; and some are master teachers, such as coaches for National Board Certification for Professional Teaching.

Expert Coaches

- One-on-one mentors—New teacher induction

- Content coaches—Literacy, math, science

- Master teacher coaches—National Board Certification

Box 7.1

Peer Coaches

Peer coaching, while dramatically different from expert coaching, provides a powerful coaching alternative that many schools are pursuing. Peer coaches come in a wide variety of sizes and shapes, just as expert coaches do. There are peer coaches that guide data-driven instructional models; e-partners for technology integration; grade level, departmental, and cross-disciplinary coaches for job-alike and/or team coaching models; and finally there are peer coaches who train together as an expert cadre who support other teachers in the building in current academic initiatives.

Peer Coaching

- Data coaches
- E-partners
- Grade level coaching
- Departmental coaches
- Cross-disciplinary coaches
- Teacher-to-teacher expert cadre

Box 7.2

Three Essential Elements

As in the designer, presenter, and facilitator roles, the role of coach has several critical aspects. Included and embedded among the three essential elements of the coaching role are the ideas of teaming, talking, and transferring. To briefly reinforce these three elements, think of the three Ts: *Teaming* is about identifying a mentor, coach, partner, or team to work with; *talking* is about carving out time to talk, dialogue, and reflect; and *transferring* is about taking the ideas to the practical level in real and purposeful applications.

Teaming . . . With a Mentor or Colleague

Creating a partnership or teaming with a mentor or colleague is the beginning of the coaching relationship. The first order of business that is paramount to everything else to come is establishing a rapport between or among those involved in the coaching scenario. Without a sound relationship or sense of camaraderie, it is difficult if not impossible to truly coach someone in the change process.

Coaching is intimate; it is dependent on getting to know each other fairly well and building a sense of integrity and trust. To do this, there are any number of encounters the coach can orchestrate with the mentee, protégé, partner,

> *The first order of business that is paramount to everything else to come is establishing a rapport.*

or team. Among the ideas for generating those encounters are three that stand out in the coach's repertoire: sharing philosophies, comparing similarities and differences, and spending informal time together.

Sharing philosophies. Sharing philosophies of education is an interesting way to create a team spirit or a sense of who the people are in the coaching relationship. Through quick conversations, the parties involved can get a real sense of the people they are working with. One may mention her need to create a classroom in which student independence is valued, while the other may respond that she prefers a somewhat more structured approach. Strict alignment of philosophies does not matter. What does matter is that these kinds of conversations begin to build a relationship.

Similarities and differences. As time together continues, there are more opportunities to find out how the team members are alike and how they are different, not only in their teaching but also in their lives. By sharing all kinds of things about oneself, the other gains insights into the partner or partners. It is only after some time together, and some moments of head-to-head, heart-to-heart talks, that any relationship begins to take off.

Once that level of conversation is established, members seem to become more committed to the coaching situation. Therefore, it behooves the person in the coaching role to have these kinds of conversations and to willingly spend some quality time becoming friends, if the coaching is to have significant impact.

Now, that doesn't mean that these conversations are apart from the coaching tasks at hand. Instead, they become part and parcel of the time together. These meaningful conversations may get more personal as time goes on and are the kinds of things one does to bond with another human being. While this may sound too touchy-feely for some, the coach who has real influence over another's performance is connected to that person. They like each other, trust each other, and have a robust respect for each other.

It is only after some time together, and some moments of head-to-head, heart-to-heart talks, that any relationship begins to take off.

Informal time together. This leads to the third interaction, informal time together. Without giving this element undo weight, as the coaching role is part of a professional relationship, the impact of having some informal time together—just to get to know each other as people rather than by formal roles each plays—can be extraordinarily significant. For whatever reasons, the opportunity to have some informal time together—at lunch, before school, after school, at another meeting, or at a school gathering— goes a long way in developing a team spirit.

These are times for the coaching team to chat about school things, but also to reveal little details about themselves. It's the perfect time to share stories about teaching experiences, establish credibility on both sides, and begin to reach out to the other party as a trusted member of the team.

To say that it is difficult to coach someone without the sense of being collaborative teammates with mutual respect would be a gross understatement. To coach, to cue, to genuinely support a colleague in professional endeavors such as curriculum alignment, instructional strategies, and sound pedagogy first requires a sense of togetherness. Then a sense develops that the two, or the team, are in this together, that they have mutual goals and objectives and mutual feelings of care and respect.

Of course, this kind of rapport builds over time, but it can be speeded up quite significantly when the coach intentionally schedules enough time to become acquainted with the colleagues in her care. Yes, some of this happens quite naturally as the team works together and develops respect for one another's talents, but it is also true that some informal time together acts as a catalyst to building a solid relationship.

Demonstrating the idea of using informal gatherings to build trust is the school faculty social committee. When several faculty members happen to be on the social committee at the same time—planning celebrations and faculty events—those team members more often than not come away from that year with a bonding to the other team members. They have had lots of time together, problem solving and planning . . . and lots of laughs together as they become friends.

Talking . . . Frequently and Regularly

Taking the opportunity to talk frequently and regularly is paramount to developing a coaching model of impact and influence. That is why a coach or a mentor needs to be home-based in the building, if possible. If the coach must travel to several buildings or across an entire district, the coach must have a published schedule of the planned time in the building.

When the teachers know when the coach is available—what he or she will be doing and where he or she will be doing it—it creates a comfort zone among all parties and a sense of the coach as an everyday part of the team. In contrast, showing up unexpectedly creates a sense of uneasiness among team members. Nobody wants to be surprised in the classroom situation. Teachers' first concerns are about their classrooms. They deserve the courtesy of a plan and a schedule within which the coaching will occur.

> *Teachers' first concerns are about their classrooms. They deserve the courtesy of a plan and a schedule*

There are several protocols that are a natural part of the coaching role to encourage regular and frequent talking. One is the coaching conference; a second is in journaling chats, and a third involves reflective dialogues about modeling and video analyses.

The coaching conference. The coaching conference is typically a cyclical model of a preconference, an observation, or visitation (walk-throughs or look-fors) and a postconference.

Preconference: In the preconference, the coaching team talks about what they will each do. They plan the interaction. Either the teacher plans a lesson or the coach plans a modeling lesson, and both leave the preconference preparing for the classroom visit.

Observation: The lesson takes place with both parties involved as planned. Eventually, either right after the lesson (which is best) or later in the day, they sit down in a postconference and debrief the entire episode. The observation is the pivot point of the postconference. It is what the two actually talk about in friendly and instructive kinds of conversations.

Postconference: Ideally, the postconference begins with a brief commentary by the teacher who has been observed. It is the moment when the learner reacts, emotionally and otherwise, to the observation from a personally relevant perspective. Once the initial reaction is presented by the learner, the debriefing is sparked by questions from the coach to the person being coached. The coach may use a series of Socratic-like questions that are reflective and probing in nature. The coach may simply ask what went well and what the teacher might do differently if she did the same lesson again. There are more metacognitive reflective tools in Tools to Use at the end of this chapter. But more often than not, it is the coach pointing out some specific things to the learner in this coaching session.

The coach may probe more deeply into the debriefing by asking why the teacher thinks or how the teacher knew something. Yet one thing is certain, to get the most out of the post-conference, both parties must participate in the talking and debriefing. It is deadly if the coach takes over the postconference and evaluates every little detail of the lesson. Coaching is a two-way street. A coach can only coach someone who is willing to be coached. Coaching must be a bilateral affair.

> A coach can only coach someone who is willing to be coached.

Observation versus opinion: To elaborate on the idea of a bilateral affair, it is often helpful for the coach to review some actual data from the observation. This is authentic data; it is what the coach sees and hears the teacher do or say. Yet this skill in observing another is both an art and a science. It takes the knowing eye of the artist to recognize the subtleties of classroom instructional practice. It takes the honed skill of a scientist to learn to distinguish between ones' opinion and one's actual observation of what happens in the classroom. It is not always easy to separate opinion and fact—what one *actually* sees and hears versus what one *thinks about* what is occurring in the classroom observation.

To illustrate the art and science of observation versus opinion (Danielson, 1996), it is often helpful for the aspiring coach or mentor to practice deciphering observable from opinionated data. For instance, by viewing videotaped lessons, or even by viewing film clips of teachers in the movies, mentors are able to practice making statements of what they see and hear rather than statements of what they think and know. A particular episode to use with the adult learner is a scene from the film *Stripes* in which the teacher is addressing a group of adults who are attending a night class to learn English. It is the scene in which the teacher asks if anyone speaks English or a little English. Just a little warning, the scene is funny, but has an adult flavor to it, so presenters must be sure to watch it prior to using it in a session.

Journals. Another powerful opportunity to "talk frequently and regularly" is often centered on a journaling experience. In the coaching scenario, the strategy of keeping a journal of some kind is critical. This reflective tool encourages the learner to think deeply about "frontline" interactions. It is in the journaling that the teacher can step back from the action and think about what has occurred. It is in the use of a journal that the teacher and the coach can actually reveal the inner workings of the complex acts of the teaching-learning scenarios.

There are many kinds of journals, as listed in Box 7.3. They range from mediated journals, in which the coach actually guides the types of entries that are made, to the reflective portfolio, in which the learner gathers artifacts of the teaching-learning episodes to reflect on and share with the coach. The authors recommend the journaling focus be changed intermittently to keep the journaling fresh and appealing to the learner. By shifting focus to a new type of journal, the protégé is more likely to be motivated to continue journaling.

Coaching With Journals

- Mediated journal
- Tiny transfer book
- Double-entry journal
- Dialogue journal
- Art journal
- Action journal
- Reflective portfolio

Box 7.3

Mediated journal: The mediated journal is one with pages that are labeled—with the guidance of the coach—for a particular focus. Each page has a heading that mediates or guides the entry focus, such as Student Responses! Best Part! Most Surprising! Needs Attention!

Tiny transfer book: A foldable little book made from a single sheet of paper is used to capture instructional strategies and teaching ideas discussed and/or modeled. The ideas are slotted for transfer and application.

Double-entry journal: A journal that is divided into two columns, one for a descriptive entry, the other for a reflective entry that relates to the description of what occurred.

Dialogue journal: This is a journal that actually is passed back and forth between the coach and the person being coached. The teacher writes an entry, and the coach responds to the entry in a written response in the same journal, literally creating a dialogue between the two.

Art journal: For those who may prefer the visual modality, an art journal can be an exciting tool for the coaching scenario. The art journal, real or virtual, consists of sketches, charts, graphs, and graphic organizers that tell the story of some aspect of the classroom interactions.

Action journal: The action journal is similar to a plan book in which the teacher plots the applications to try, as discussed and agreed on with the coach. It is a map or reminder of what the teacher wants to try or include in her teaching before the next visit with the coach.

Reflective portfolio: A reflective portfolio is a collection of artifacts, that is, student work samples or teacher planning tools. Each artifact in the portfolio contains a description and a reflection by the teacher.

Reflective dialogues. Another protocol for "frequent and regular talking" is in the reflective analyses of teaching episodes or in examining student work. In both cases, there are actual or videotaped versions of the teacher teaching, the coach modeling, or student learning. These authentic examples provide fertile ground for reflection and analysis that can lead to improved instruction and increased student achievement.

Actual or videotaped teaching or model lesson: This can be an analysis that follows a videotape or an actual teaching or modeling episode. In either case, it provides fertile ground for reflection and debriefing that has a laser-like focus. Using a video segment of an actual lesson executed either by the teacher or by the coach offers real footage for them to look over and analyze in detail. The videos serve as authentic learning experiences offering powerful opportunities for in-depth analysis.

Both viewers have a point of view, and so the discussions that ensue can be enlightening and insightful. The video analysis requires some level of sophistication in the coaching relationship—and some level of trust. If such trust occurs at this stage of the coaching, these talking sessions can be one of the most fruitful.

Examining student work: In addition to the video analysis of a lesson or the debriefing of a model lesson, an exciting reflective discussion occurs via the exercise of examining student work. When looking over actual student work artifacts, both the coach and teacher have a window into the student and his or her learning. These authentic examples provide the necessary data to make critical decisions about instructional interventions.

For example, in one instance the coach advised the teacher to provide the constructed response section of the sampled reading test in a 2-day cycle. On the first day, the kids would take the test, on their own, exactly as in the testing situation, and they would write their responses in pencil. On the second day, the teacher would revisit the same sample test questions and debrief with the students by giving them the corrected and completed responses. The students would then add these to their pencil responses but write them in red pen. Then the coach and the teacher would analyze the papers and dissect the weaknesses in the student responses, looking for patterns or trends. Areas needing improvement would become the target of the instructional interventions for the next round. Such a process of analysis creates a robust reflection activity for both the teacher and the coach.

Transferring . . . to Classroom Applications

Seven strategies to foster transfer from the staff room to the classroom. "Coaching for transfer" is the name of the game in professional learning. There are seven research-based strategies (Fogarty & Pete, 2004b) that seem to foster transfer from staff room training to classroom instruction. These strategies are listed in Box 7.4. Moving from awareness and understanding about transfer and application to a set of protocols that promote transfer (setting expectations, plotting an application, and committing to try something immediately), the following discussion emphasizes that transfer works when, and only when, it is an integral focus of professional development. Each of the seven strategies is discussed more fully in the following discussion, as the transfer and application plan unfolds.

> *"Coaching for transfer" is the name of the game in professional learning.*

Seven Transfer Strategies

1. Learn about transfer theory

2. Set expectations for transfer

3. Model with authentic artifacts

4. Reflect on levels of transfer

5. Plot applications with the tiny transfer book

6. Try something immediately

7. Dialogue with hugging/bridging questions

Box 7.4

1. Learn About Transfer Theory

The first important protocol to foster transfer from the staff room to the classroom is learning about transfer theory. Some basic facts offer insight into this phenomenon. They include knowing about the evolution of the theory itself and the two major types of transfer that appear in the literature.

Transfer theory: The theory of transfer has evolved over time. There are three significant phases that have occurred: the Bo Peep Phase, the Black Sheep Phase, and the Good Shepherd Phase (Perkins & Solomon, 1987). Each has helped to shed some light on the idea of transfer.

The *Bo Peep Phase* of transfer basically mirrors the belief captured in the nursery rhyme, Little Bo Peep: "Leave them alone, and they'll come home, wagging their tails behind them." In essence, the belief states that if you teach well, with rigor and skill, students will learn. For example, in the early days of transfer theory, the idea of teaching geometry and Latin to all students as ways to "train the mind" was alive and well.

Training the mind, in classical education terms, generally meant to develop critical and creative thinking skills for life through specific exercises required in learning the rarely spoken language of Latin and in constructing the theoretical understandings of geometric theorems in geometry class. Just teach well and they will learn and in turn naturally transfer that learning to all areas of life. This phase gave way to the next.

Even more elusive, the *Black Sheep Phase* generated the theory that transfer was the metaphorical black sheep of the family of teaching and learning. Transfer became the skeleton in the closet, the crazy aunt in the attic. No one seemed to know very much about the concept, its elusive cause, or what to do about it, so the transfer concept became the unspoken secret of the academic community. In fact, there was a period when very little was researched or written about the transfer of learning. It disappeared from the academic world of research and writing.

By contrast, the *Good Shepherd Phase,* presented by Perkins and Solomon (1987), offers hope and insight into the theory of transfer. Explained briefly, this phase reflects the belief that if teachers or trainers "shepherd" transfer, if they pay attention to transfer and keep it in their sights, if they treat it like prized sheep and continually monitor and keep it within the parameters of the "herd," transfer will not only survive, it will thrive. In brief, transfer will flourish when it becomes part and parcel of the training model and when it is paid as much attention as the initial teaching-learning stages. And this is where the phase rests currently.

Two types of transfer: There are two types of transfer referenced in the literature. One is simple transfer, close in context to the original learning, and the other is complex transfer, remote and far from the context of the initial learning. Each of these types is handled differently when trying to foster or promote transfer of learning.

The first, *simple transfer,* occurs very near the original learning. The transfer required is similar, and the situation is not that far removed from the first learning. The transfer is so close, in fact, that it is almost automatic. A common example of simple transfer is driving. Once one has learned to drive a car, driving a rental truck is not that different. The transfer is almost automatic, although driving a truck may require a bit more attention than driving a car.

Simple transfer may be achieved when the learning in the new situation "hugs" (Perkins & Solomon, 1987) the learning in the original situation. The more students practice a skill, the more automatic the transfer of that skill becomes. When children practice their times tables, they find it quite easy to automatically transfer the information when solving a math-related problem. The skill is on autopilot!

The second kind of transfer is *complex transfer,* or transfer that is far removed from the original learning. The transfer is not automatic or natural. Instead, it requires mindfulness and careful consideration. Complex transfer requires "bridging" (Perkins & Solomon, 1987) from one scenario to another. It is necessary to think about how to use the skill or the learning in the new context.

Learning about argument and evidence offers an example of complex transfer. As a youngster, one argues with a sibling in unending cycles. Neither understands the formal model of providing evidence to support the argument, even though they may inadvertently give reasons for their point of view. Yet when learning about how to write a persuasive essay, all they know about authentic arguments goes to the wind. Students may take a point of view and then form an argument to persuade others of the worth of their opinion. However, learning how to provide sound details in the form of supporting evidence is often not done intuitively, as when arguing with a brother, but rather consciously and explicitly, as when a student learns to write a persuasive essay with three supporting details. The process is formal, mindful, somewhat deliberate, and possibly laborious.

In summary, both kinds of transfer, simple and complex, are part of professional learning. Staff developers, of course, need to "hug" and "bridge" learning if they are to promote transfer.

2. Set Expectations for Transfer

One of the most important elements for fostering the transfer of learning is in the early stages of the training when the trainer sets the expectation for transfer. While transfer is expected as a natural outcome of computer software training, for example, it is not always an expected outcome of educational professional development experiences. Many times teachers attend conferences, seminars, or workshops with no mandate to bring anything away. There is often no explicit expectation for immediate and practical transfer to their work setting.

To set expectations for transfer and application, trainers often use specific tools and techniques. Two that immediately come to mind are the Take Away Window and the Tiny Transfer Book. Of course, there are many other ideas for promoting transfer and application back in the classroom, but these are two that seem to work best.

Take Away Window: The trainer tells participants right up front that they are going to acquire lots of good ideas to use immediately in their classrooms or work settings. These skillful staff developers set expectations early on. Then, they actually create a "take away window," or list of strategies, concepts, and skills that are covered in the workshop. Trainers and participants continually add to the list and reference the ideas, asking participants to think about how they might use them in their classrooms.

Transfer Book: The Tiny Transfer Book is another tool participants use to capture ideas from the workshop. Each time a new strategy or skill is introduced, the trainers remind participants to jot the idea down in their tiny transfer book. Then, they are coached to think of a relevant application for their particular subject area grade level. They are cautioned to ask for help if they are not seeing practical, meaningful connections to their work. When that is the case, the staff developer helps brainstorm ideas for relevant applications. If there is a three-day workshop, there are three tiny transfer books, one for each day. It is a marvelously simple little tool that gets lots of mileage for conveying ideas from the workshop back to the classroom.

3. Model With Authentic Artifacts

One of the most helpful ways to encourage relevant transfer and application of ideas, strategies, and skills to the actual K–12 classroom is to demonstrate the various kinds of applications others have made. By collecting real and diverse samples of student and teacher artifacts, the staff developer can spark further applications within the training setting. These artifacts may be saved and shown or photographed and scanned for showing in an electronic version.

Student artifacts: Student artifacts range from writing samples and math problems that have been solved to complete portfolios of student work on an entire unit. By viewing different examples from elementary, middle, and high school levels, participants can relate more easily to the applications. By sharing math, social studies, language arts, and science examples, participants again have the advantage of near transfer and can more easily see the connections to their content and their students. By gathering a vast number of artifacts and demonstrating a variety of applications, participants too may see possible uses of an idea.

Teacher artifacts: Teacher artifacts are equally powerful catalysts for transfer, especially in training situations because participants can actually see how other teachers have used a strategy in their classrooms. Teacher artifacts span the spectrum from standards-based lessons and integrated units to specific applications of thinking skills to demonstrations of a literacy lesson. These shared artifacts are one of the most powerful ways to entice teachers to actively apply a transfer strategy.

Modeling or demonstrating: In addition, the staff developer may model teaching behaviors, using videotaped sequences to demonstrate a strategy or even film clips of Hollywood movies to underscore a point.

4. Reflect on Levels of Transfer

There are six levels of transfer that are easily recognizable in most professional development or coaching situations for adult learners. These include progressive stages of overlooking transfer, duplicating the idea exactly, replicating the idea by changing something, integrating the idea with an existing repertoire, mapping the ideas to use in specific ways, and innovating creatively with an idea to take it above and beyond the original idea.

Using a set of bird metaphors, these six levels of transfer are described more fully in Box 7.5. The metaphors include *Ollie, Head in the Sand Ostrich; Dan, the Drilling Woodpecker; Laura, the Look-Alike Penguin; Jonathan Livingston Seagull; Cathy, the Carrier Pigeon; and Sam, the Soaring Eagle.*

Levels of Transfer

- **Ollie,** Head-in-the-Sand Ostrich, overlooks the opportunity to use the new idea.
- **Dan,** the Drilling Woodpecker, duplicates, copies exactly as it is learned.
- **Laura,** the Look-Alike Penguin, replicates by tailoring slightly to fit needs.
- **Jonathan Livingston,** the Seagull, integrates subtly, into existing repertoire.
- **Cathy,** the Carrier Pigeon, maps (propagates) the idea intentionally and deliberately.
- **Sam,** the Soaring Eagle, innovates and invents marvelous applications.

Box 7.5

Ollie, Head in the Sand Ostrich, overlooks the opportunity to use the new idea. Ollie overlooks the application, either intentionally or unintentionally. In either case, Ollie does nothing with the idea and seems unaware of its relevance. Ollie sometimes chooses not to use an idea because it seems counterproductive to him and thus becomes determined not to use the idea. In short, Ollie misses the opportunity for appropriate applications and never really uses the ideas back in the classroom. Like Ollie, teachers may learn about how to use data to inform their practice in the classroom but never actually go back to their school and use data in that way.

Dan, the Drilling Woodpecker, duplicates, copies exactly as it is learned. Dan duplicates the idea exactly as it has been presented. In fact, many times Dan will actually ask the presenter if he may have a copy of the strategy or skill used in the workshop. Dan drills and practices again and again. Drill! Drill! Drill! Then he stops. In essence, Dan uses the idea as a single-minded activity, not as a strategy that can be used, reused, and then used again, all in different situations and different ways. Yet this is an early level of simple transfer and must be applauded because the teacher is leaving the workshop with an idea to take back and use. One example of this level of transfer is when an eager teacher asks for copies of the scoring rubrics shown as examples during the workshop.

Laura, the Look-Alike Penguin, replicates by tailoring slightly to fit needs. Laura replicates the skill or strategy by tailoring it to her students or her content. She tends to apply it in the same way, however, once she has slightly customized it to fit those needs. She uses very similar kinds of applications over and over again, never really branching out more creatively. Like a string of penguins, all her applications seem to look alike. Laura just does not transfer the idea into different situations. Her transfer, however, is both real and practical, as it fits her specific circumstances, so Laura should be commended for that. One example of Laura's tailoring may be found in her using a concept map by mapping the plot of a story. Although Laura may change the story, she never uses the concept map for any other applications other than story plots.

Jonathan Livingston Seagull integrates subtly into existing repertoire. Jonathan often says, "I already do this." Like Jonathan, the teacher subtly integrates this strategy into his or her classroom with a raised consciousness about it and its use. This teacher has an acute awareness of the strategy and a renewed interest in it. In fact, he or she may use the strategy with deliberate refinement and skillful integration. The strategy is blended into an existing repertoire and never considered a new idea but rather an old idea revisited. Bloom's taxonomy of questions is an example of this kind of strategy. Teachers often think they know it and use it, so when it is introduced into a session, they recognize it as a familiar strategy.

Cathy, the Carrier Pigeon, maps (propagates) the idea intentionally and deliberately. Cathy is an eager and proactive participant who actively maps ideas across her content or grade level. This teacher propagates ideas and takes them from one application to another, consciously transferring ideas to various situations and content areas. This level of transfer is characterized by a teacher who carries the strategy to various situations as part of his available repertoire. One example of this is the teacher who learns about the multiple-intelligences approach to learning and maps the use of these intelligences into various lessons throughout the unit.

Sam, the Soaring Eagle, innovates and invents marvelous applications. Sam is a risk taker who finds innovative ways to use the new strategy. This level of transfer shows evidence of "flying with an idea" and putting ideas into action. It demonstrates how applications may go beyond the initial conception and create truly inventive uses for the idea. Sam enhances, invents, and diverges from the initial idea, fully achieving its full value. To illustrate this level of transfer, a teacher might learn about higher-order thinking skills, and instead of simply using them with her students, she also charges them with the task of identifying the kinds of higher-order thinking an author exhibits in his writing. This is far above the original idea of using higher-order thinking in classroom interactions.

5. Plot Applications With the Tiny Transfer Book

The idea of plotting an application is explicit and direct. The trainer guides this process and coaches the teacher to find a meaningful application before the teacher ever leaves the training site. Getting teachers to commit to an application is half the battle. If the teacher has a good idea about how to use the strategy, then perhaps that teacher will be moved to actually go back and use it.

6. Try Something Immediately

The next step once the teacher has plotted an application idea is to get the teacher to go back and do something immediately. The sooner the teacher tries something, the greater the chance for real and meaningful transfer. By creating application buddies or partners and requiring an action plan, the staff developer raises the likelihood of transfer. A verbal or other commitment to another teacher often generates enough power to compel the teacher to actually try something.

7. Dialogue With Hugging/Bridging Questions

The use of dialoguing questions goes hand in hand with the transfer buddy idea. By creating peer partners early in the year by means of always sending two or more people to trainings so they have a partner to work with, by encouraging conversation and sharing about new ideas, transfer is more likely to occur. Also, by instructing teachers about the levels of transfer, as depicted in number four above, and coaching them on how to dialogue about their own transfer, the trainer makes this reflective dialogue a key component of professional development. The following examples, in Form 7.1, illustrate the dialoguing questions that spark transfer.

Form 7.1 Dialogue With Hugging and Bridging Strategies

Overlooking

Think of an instance when the skill or strategy would not be appropriate.

I would not use (the skill or strategy) when . . .

Duplicating

Think of an "opportunity passed," when you could have used the skill or strategy.

I wish I'd known about . . .

when . . .

Replicating

Think of an adjustment that will make your application of _____ more relevant.

Next time I'm gonna . . .

Integrating

Think of an analogy for the skill or strategy.

_____ *is like*_____*because both . . .*

Propagating

Think of an opportunity to use the new ideas.

*Next*_____*, I could use* _____*when . . .*

Innovating

Think of an application for a real-life setting.

*I could use*_____*when . . .*

Figure 7.1   Coaching Role Rubric (to be completed by the reader)

	Developing	Competent	Proficient	Exceptional
Teaming With a Mentor	(Meeting)	(Sharing)	(Planning)	(Doing)
Talking Frequently and Regularly	(Survival)	(Instructional)	(Insightful)	(Transforming)
Transferring to Classroom Applications	(Applied)	(Integrated)	(Embedded)	(Trade marked)

TOOLS TO USE ■

1. Metacognitive Reflection Tools (see references in Chapter 6)

Mr. Parnes's Questions

Mrs. Potter's Questions

Ms. Poindexter

Dial 4-1-1

3-2-1

Yellow Brick Road

Human Graph

Tiny Transfer Book

Take Away Window

What? So, what? Now, what?

2. Seven Transfer Strategies

1. Learn about transfer theory
2. Set expectations for transfer
3. Model with authentic artifacts
4. Reflect on levels of transfer
5. Plot applications with the tiny transfer book
6. Try something immediately
7. Dialogue with hugging/bridging questions

3. Coaching Tools (listen, build trust, help plan, cheer on, provide resources)

Response Journals

Double-Entry Journals

Book Studies

Partner Work

Group Work

Virtual Groups
    Online Courses: e-partners
    Introductory Level
    Supportive Level

Visitations/Observations
    Classrooms
    Schools

Conferences
    Walk-Throughs/Look-Fors

Magic Book

1. Each person needs two single sheets of 8.5 × 11 paper.

2. Fold the first sheet in half (hamburger style) and tear the sheet in half.

3. Save one half and tear it in half again, making two strips of equal length and width. Save the two strips and put the half aside.

4. Take the second whole sheet of paper and fold it in half like a hamburger bun fold.

5. Then, fold both sides back toward the fold creating wings or the letter "w" if you look at it from the end.

6. Grasp the middle section of the same piece of paper between the two wings and mark off two spots to create thirds.

7. Now, tear the two marked spots through the fold to the mark. When you are done the paper should look like three teeth.

8. Now, open the torn paper and weave the two strips through the sections on each side.

9. After the weaving is done, fold the book together with the six sections in the middle, giving it a good crease.

10. Carefully find the middle and open to these six sections; close it again.

11. Carefully find the two edges beneath the six-sectioned middle and pull those far edges out to see the big "magic" page hidden behind the six sections.

12. The Magic Book is ready for the note-taking activity.

4. T-Chart Activity

Read the following synopsis in Box 7.7 and create a T-chart (Figure 7.2) to operationalize the role of coach in the field. Tell specifically what it looks and sounds like when the staff developer is in the role of mediator or coach in the field.

Coach Role

Team participants to build trusting relationships for job-embedded peer coaching and sustained applications that structure for success.

Talk is structured through dialogue and articulation opportunities that foster reflective practices.

Transfer is promoted through explicit strategies for immediate, relevant, and meaningful applications in the classroom.

Box 7.7

Figure 7.2   Coaching Role: T-Chart

Looks Like	Sounds Like
Specifically what the staff developer does	Specifically what the staff developer says

8

A Guide to the Anatomy of a Workshop

Vignette: Don't Waste My Time

One of the most discouraging things for the staff developer who has put time, effort, and energy into a workshop design is to hear a stray negative comment that sometimes jumpstarts the consultant's day. Overheard more than once at the training room door are the following laments from reluctant participants:

"I don't even know why I'm here!"

"I'd rather work in my room!"

"I'm so tired of these workshops that go nowhere. They're never any help to me in the classroom."

"I brought my work with me."

Hearing these or similar comments, one principal decided to do something different. She created the Staff Development Advisory Team, which elicited input from grade levels and departments. Starting with a structured list of topics that supported their goals, teachers decided by areas on the professional development focus that they needed. By obtaining their opinions in a "forced-choice" method, she was able to generate more buy-in and ownership.

While on the right track, the principal needed to know about another key to changing these negatives to positives. According to Joyce and Showers (2002), the success or failure of a workshop lies in the design. Meeting participant needs, of course, is a big part of that successful design.

Yet another key component to a successful professional development experience is embedded in what is labeled here as "the anatomy of the workshop." Turning such negative comments into rave reviews is indeed possible. When the design of the training includes four critical elements, successful professional learning is not only possible but almost guaranteed. So just what are these elements? Staff developers can examine the anatomy of a workshop more closely as they read this chapter to see what this claim is all about.

After all, wouldn't a staff developer prefer to hear words such as these:

"Great day! I learned so much that I can use right away."

"This was so relevant."

"I can't wait to get back to my class to try these ideas."

"I really feel renewed."

"What a day! I'm overwhelmed with good ideas. I don't know where to start."

THE TRAINING MODEL THAT WORKS ■

Understanding that the four prior chapters elaborate on the design of the workshop, the presentation, facilitation, and the coaching skills of the trainer, this chapter extends the concept of an anatomy of a workshop. The focus of this chapter is the research on the training model from Joyce and Showers (2002), in which they lay out the four elements that seem to be absolutely necessary for successful training experiences.

This discussion focuses on the research-based best practices in the actual training model. As depicted in Figure 8.1, the inverted triangle suggests the concept of drilling deep within the various aspects of working with adult learners. The figure begins with the broadest concept of adult learning and change, narrows to the next concept of professional development, and finally terminates with the most focused concept of the actual training. The reader may want to take a moment to reflect on the sequence in the figure.

Leading voices in the field of training are Bruce Joyce and Beverly Showers. Their research highlights the critical elements of effective training. In their classic text, *Student Achievement Through Staff Development* (2002), they were among the first to discuss that elusive link between staff development activities in the staff room and increased student achievement in the classroom. They make that seemingly obvious connection that often eludes other educators leading

Leading voices in the field of training are Bruce Joyce and Beverly Showers.

Figure 8.1   Some Things We Know

the change process. For them, it's all too common that some type of professional development happens, yet there is no explicit expectation for positive results in terms of increased student achievement. Although the implicit goal is most certainly to realize change in student learning, success in making an actual connection to that goal is not always achieved.

As this discussion unfolds, the training work of Joyce and Showers is the engine that runs the change train. Their well-known model, revered by staff developers throughout the educational community, includes four major elements: theory, demonstration, practice, and coaching. Their training model is at the heart of the change process as initiatives are introduced into schools. Before proceeding, the reader may want to take a minute to rank the four elements according to the impact each has on professional development.

Each of the four elements is fully discussed separately. Box 8.1 shows the weight each element carries in the overall process and provides an easy comparison of the various elements as the reader analyzes the entirety of the training model.

The Training Model

Include THEORY	0% transfer in the classroom
And, add a DEMONSTRATION	0% transfer in the classroom
And, provide PRACTICE	0% transfer in the classroom
And, require on-site COACHING	95% transfer in the classroom

Box 8.1

Theory

The first element is theory. Good sound professional development establishes the theory base for the initiative by reviewing the research that supports the ideas manifested in the initiative. The theory becomes the scholarly citations that undergird the change initiative that is the focus of the training.

Attention to theory is basic to the change process.

Attention to theory is basic to the change process.

The theory base of research studies provides needed rationale for the change initiative. The theory is what ultimately sparks the hope and optimism that change will create the intended difference in the targeted situation.

Although the element of theory is an integral part of the overall training model, it need not be the lead piece in the training. In fact, it usually is more effective to integrate the theory into the training a bit later in the process, after participants have some level of understanding about the actual initiative. Skillful trainers have a sixth sense about when it seems timely to introduce the theory base. In addition, they seem to sense what, when, and how much the group needs and/or wants in terms of the theoretical underpinnings of the initiative and act accordingly.

Perhaps a brief example of the impact that the theory portion of a training experience can have on participants will help underscore its importance. In Melbourne, Australia, the master of ceremonies of the Brain Conference kicked off the training with a short but telling introduction of the keynote speaker, Howard Gardner, the founder and developer of the highly acclaimed theory of multiple intelligences. The emcee announced, "I'd like to introduce you to Howard Gardner, the man who started it all when he added an *s* to the word *intelligence*." As he finished, it was as quiet as a church service in the auditorium of 800 people. That was just what they wanted to hear. They were there for the theory—straight from the horse's mouth!

Demonstration

"Your actions speak so loudly, I can't hear your words" is an old adage that rings true in the training world. The demonstration is the action shot, the modeling that speaks loudly and clearly to all involved. The demonstration element is presented in any number of formats: live, face-to-face modeling; video clips of modeled behaviors; or the display and discussion of authentic artifacts.

Your actions speak so loudly, I can't hear your words.

The demonstration portion of the training, as with theory, is best when woven into the training. Sometimes beginning the session with a demonstration of the target behavior is most effective. At other times, blending demonstrations into the heart of the training material immediately following an explanation of the behavior is more appropriate.

On other occasions, the flow of the training material may dictate that demonstrations be used toward the end of the presentation, as a conclusion to the discussion that ensued.

However, regardless of timing, demonstrations are essential to training. This is the operational component that models the theory with real examples, showing what the initiative looks and sounds like. This is the story of how it works, not just the declaration that it does work. The demonstration is the authentic look at the initiative in action, and sometimes that action is modeled in myriad ways to fully illustrate its effectiveness in various scenarios.

A quick example of the power of the demonstration element is illustrated in this story about a cooperative learning initiative. After four full days of training with a theory base and lots of interactive experiences in the sessions, participants revealed a startling fact: many still did not know how they would go back to their schools and implement cooperative learning groups in their classrooms! In response to this concern, one of the leaders suggested watching a homegrown video on cooperative learning. She explained that three teachers had videotaped their first cooperative learning lessons as models for other teachers in their school. To make a long story short (if it's not too late), the video showed three different classrooms (first, fourth, and sixth grades) with three different cooperative learning lessons. Each lesson clip was only about four to five minutes in length, yet the response from the training group was absolutely astonishing. Participants sighed with relief and said to each other and to the leaders, "Oh, we can do that. We know exactly what to do now after seeing cooperative groups in action." That's the power of a good demonstration!

Practice

Practice makes perfect? No, practice makes permanent! Or, perfect practices makes perfect. Training with only theory and demonstrations—no matter how powerful—seldom yields relevant transfer or authentic applications that have true and long lasting impact.

Practice makes perfect? No, practice makes permanent! Or, perfect practices makes perfect.

Participants become empowered to actually use the information in their home settings when they have some amount of guided practice during the training itself. Practice might be somewhat contrived—perhaps using simulations or role playing—abbreviated in terms of actual time needed—and perhaps even sampled through one generic application. But practice has to take place, and participants must immerse themselves in actual trials of the initiative. They must experience the process, have opportunities to ask questions, and have their concerns addressed. They need some hands-on time with the skills and strategies to get the feel of the process, to operationalize abstract theory and have an opportunity to experience what it actually looks and sounds like.

As mentioned earlier, a colleague attended a day-long software training in the ballroom of a local hotel, he was astonished to find that he was one of 450 other participants. They were seated at long tables, with no computers and no keyboards. The session included a software demonstration, projected onto the 12×12 screen, with a running monologue of the procedure. Participants were expected to make notes in their three-ring binders, with some questions allowed during the presentation. Yet because there was no hands-on component possible in this setting, the learner left frustrated and unsure about how to actually use the complicated software package.

Coaching

Coaching is the onsite follow-up. It resembles feedback, but the difference is that coaching takes place on the job. It is job embedded. This ongoing, on-site coaching may consist of experts coaching novices or peers coaching each other. Yet in either case, there is opportunity for immediate, specific refinement to the learner's performance. The coach provides the mirror to the adult learner and reflects professionally on the various elements of the performance. Coaching in professional development is just like coaching in sports. It is someone telling someone else what is working and what is not. Coaching is the key to improving.

> With coaching, transfer has an astonishingly good chance of occurring.

Coaching is sometimes considered the icing or the trimming on the cake, if you will, that adds extra charm to the overall product. But it is not just the icing on the cake. It is the very element that makes the cake rise! Coaching is a fundamental element in a good training model. Without coaching, training does not take—it just does not work. Without coaching, the chances of any real application are slim at best. With coaching, transfer has an astonishingly good chance of occurring.

Box 8.1, The Training Model, makes the point. It dramatically demonstrates through data the critical difference in training with and without a coaching element. If this chart is correct—and the authors have confidence that it is—then the undeniable conclusion becomes crystal clear. No training for professional development should ever occur if coaching is not available. Coaching must be required follow-up as an integral and necessary part to the entire process of change. The evidence is just too obvious. Without coaching, there is very little possibility of meaningful transfer and application. Training without coaching is simply a waste of time and money. Coaching is the critical link from the training site to the home site, be it classroom or business office.

A CLASSIC EXAMPLE ■

A classic example comes to mind that illustrates the skill and the finesse it takes to be an effective coach. While visiting New Zealand and working on the North Island by Lake Taupo, one of the consultants on the team expressed his desire to try bungee jumping at the Taupo Bungee Jump by the river. What ensued is a perfect story to demonstrate the power of the coach. And it was all captured on the videotape they provide at the site.

As the consultant entered the area, he was weighed by the attendant, who immediately inked the number on the back of the jumper's hand. Once this was done, the jumper was quickly ushered on to the ramp area, through the barriers, and toward the jump site. At this point, two workers checked the number on his hand, adjusted the bungee, and secured the collars around the ankles of his feet. The entire time this was occurring, the one guy continued to talk to the potential jumper, giving him the vital information about how best to make the jump.

"When you're ready to jump, move toward the edge of the ramp and just fall forward. Don't worry about anything; just let gravity take you over and experience the feel of the bungee taking hold. Be careful on the bounce not to let the rope hit you. Are you ready?"

"Yep, I'm as ready as I'll ever be," and the jumper shuffled his way to the edge of the platform.

As he stood over the end looking down at the river about 190 meters below, he muttered, almost incomprehensively, "What am I doing?"

Then he stepped back a fraction of a step and said, "I don't think I can do this." Slowly, he moved back and sat down on the bench where he had been prepped a few minutes earlier.

At this point the "coach" came over to him and said, gently, "You don't have to do this if you choose not to."

Then in a loud and strong voice he said, "But, if you really want to jump, and I think you do, I know you can do it. Just stand up, walk to the edge and lean forward. Don't think about it. If you think about it, you won't do it. That's the Maori wisdom. Don't think. Just go to the edge and jump."

With that, the jumper stood up, walked the few steps directly to the edge, leaned forward, and was out of sight in an instant.

Looking over the wall, his friends saw him bounce once very high and then gradually bounce up and down a number of times before the rescue boat moved in place directly underneath the hanging jumper.

The coach had done his job well. He had

The coach was there to coach!

expressed his confidence in the jumper and instructed him in clear and concise terms exactly how to proceed. And the jumper did exactly as he had been told. The coach did a perfect job of coaching for success. And, the coach did what all good coaches are there to do. The coach was there to coach!

■   TOOLS TO USE

1. Likert Scale

Use a Likert Scale and rank the four training elements:

Theory	1	2	3	4	5	6	7	8	9	10
Demonstration	1	2	3	4	5	6	7	8	9	10
Practice	1	2	3	4	5	6	7	8	9	10
Coaching	1	2	3	4	5	6	7	8	9	10

2. Right-Angle Thinking: One of Four Elements

Use the graphic organizer, Right-Angle Thinking (Figure 8.2.), to describe and reflect on one of the four critical elements of the training model. In this right-angle thinking graphic, select one element: theory, demonstration, practice, or coaching.

The goal of this graphic organizer is to capture the stray thoughts that often occur as one is thinking about a targeted idea. The theory implies that many of these extraneous thoughts may be as important as anything else going on in the mind that seems more directly related to the target idea. Yet, those other thoughts may indeed hold some insight that is as important as the description of the known.

3. Personal Coaching Story: Tell One! Write One!

Take a moment to recall a coaching situation that you experienced in your life and use it as a parallel to the concept of coaching for transfer in professional learning situations. Describe in detail exactly what the coach said and did that seemed to help you move forward, or at least move along. This may be a formal coach who may have impacted your life or an informal coaching situation in which someone gave you the support and nudge you needed along your learning curve.

Figure 8.2 Right-Angle Thinking: Coaching

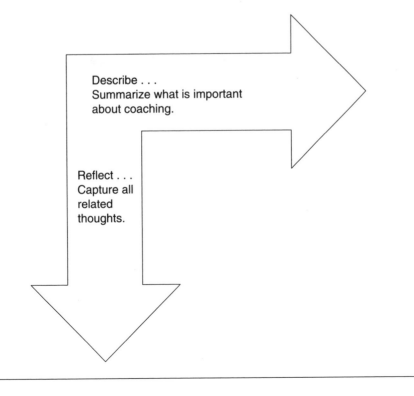

Describe . . .
Summarize what is important about coaching.

Reflect . . .
Capture all related thoughts.

9

A Guide to Sustained Professional Learning

Learning thrives when the conditions are right... with consistency, with continuity, and with a coveted commitment.

Learning thrives when the support is there... with consistency, with continuity, and with a coveted commitment.

Learning thrives when someone cares... with consistency, with continuity, and with a coveted commitment.

Learning thrives when someone is gently pushed... with consistency, with continuity, and with a coveted commitment.

—*Robin Fogarty and Brian Pete, 2006*

PROFESSIONAL LEARNING COMMUNITIES ■

A Model for Mentoring Our Teachers: Centers of Pedagogy

There is a model for mentoring all teachers. Professional learning communities may be called "centers of pedagogy" (Goodlad, 1983; Fogarty, 2001e). These centers are comprised of a team of teachers in a building with a sense of community, a sense of spirit, and a sense of collaboration. They are centers of expertise and encouragement, of experience and excitement, of empathy and energy. The centers of pedagogy offer a model for mentoring all teachers, from those just beginning to career teachers at every stage of their professional development. Centers of pedagogy is an idea whose time has come for our school faculty teams.

> *There is a model for mentoring all teachers.*

Teachers: Coming and Going

A demographic phenomenon called the "sandwich effect" is influencing school faculties across the United States and Canada. The sandwich effect is a metaphor that depicts districts with a large number of senior staff and an equally large number of beginning staff but very few teachers between because of reduction-in-force policies in intervening years.

> *A demographic phenomenon called the "sandwich effect" is influencing school faculties.*

That demographic, however, is about to change quite radically. In fact, the trend is already apparent. Predictions made in 1999 suggest that 2.5 million new teachers will enter the profession during the next 10 years. Young people right out of college as well as second-career people are being enticed to come into the field to fill needed positions. While these new teachers are entering the field, the baby boomers are reaching retirement age. The noticeable exodus of veteran teachers, which has already begun, continues at a steady rate.

To complicate matters even more for schools trying to recruit, orient, and mentor new staff, the statistics on new teacher retention are not very promising. Within the first three or four years, 25–30 percent of beginning teachers leave the ranks of the profession.

Within the first three or four years, 25–30 percent of beginning teachers leave the ranks of the profession.

They simply decide not to stay in the field, choosing to make career moves elsewhere. Thus, these desperately needed faculty members are on staff for a very short time. This situation coupled with the exodus of seniors creates an escalating teacher shortage that is just beginning to affect our schools.

Based on these projections, schools are frantically recruiting new teachers to meet their faculty needs. In an effort to provide immediate and ongoing support for these new recruits, schools often offer new teacher induction programs. By formalizing the structure of the orientation and development of new teachers, schools attempt to retain their newest staff members for the long run.

Often, a significant element in these support programs is the assignment to the beginning teacher of a mentor who provides immediate, consistent, and continual guidance to ensure his or her success. However, with changing demographics, there are already signs that there are too many new teachers and too few mentors.

A Place Called School *Revisited*

Understanding the dire need for professional development programs that mentor, coach, and provide consistent and continual support for new teachers, educational leaders are looking for innovative models for mentoring. There is a model for mentoring our teachers that exists in theory and is just beginning to appear more frequently in formal practice. Thus, this is not an entirely new idea, really, but rather a second generation of a mental model that has been around for a while.

In his influential book, *A Place Called School,* John Goodlad (1983) wrote about two concepts that seem to be natural links for a robust mentoring model for our teachers. As he talked about curriculum and instruction, he envisioned "centers of pedagogy" and "teams of teachers." First, he described *centers of pedagogy:*

> I recommend the creation of centers designed to give long term attention to research and development in school curricula and accompanying pedagogy. . . . Each center's sphere of activity would embrace an entire domain of knowledge, thought and process, . . . addressing the full scope of K–12 curriculum, . . . seeking to identify its organizing elements, . . . to suggest ways of involving students. . . . Some [centers] might be located in major universities. (p. 293)

Then Goodlad (1983) described how he envisioned creating teams of teachers within school faculties:

> [I] recommend the employment of head teachers . . . [with] highly successful teaching experience coupled with a doctorate in the field. . . . The head teachers would teach part of the time, . . . serve as role models to fellow teachers, provide in-service assistance, [and] diagnose knotty learning problems. . . . I envision them serving as heads of teaching teams made up of qualified full-time and part-time teachers, neophytes, . . . and aides. (p. 302)

By combining these two ideas—centers of pedagogy and teams of teachers—a model for mentoring our teachers emerges. The model presented here takes its name from Goodlad's vision and is referred to simply as "centers of pedagogy." The name evokes a sense of rigor and the aura of academe that speaks to the kind of rich quality envisioned for our schools.

In retrospect, this model seems quite sensible, given the impact of the sandwich effect. Why not elicit the expertise of all available faculty? Why not form a "mosaic of mentors," as Lieberman (1988) calls it? Why not explicitly recognize spheres of influence that extend naturally from professors and doctoral students at the university to teacher leaders on school faculties to master teachers and skillful practitioners to beginning peers and caring colleagues? Why not create genuine, real-life scenarios of communities of learners? Why not endorse centers of pedagogy that can influence every stage of teaching for beginning to developing to masterful teachers?

A Model for Coaching and Mentoring All Teachers

These centers of pedagogy would be comprised of five to eight teachers in a building, spanning career stages from novice to master teacher. The team composition might be decided by the principal, the faculty, or a combination of both. Perhaps the principal selects the "head teacher" that Goodlad (1983) refers to, and then staff members sort themselves into diverse teams. Or teams might already exist that would work well as centers of pedagogy.

In fact, there are several scenarios that seem ripe for a transition into centers. One large elementary school has nine first grade teachers ranging from beginning to seasoned. This creates a natural center because teachers already have time scheduled to meet as a grade to plan and share. Another faculty team scenario that exists is found in some middle schools. Teams of teachers and clusters of kids are in place in various "houses" or "families," often arranged by grade levels and across disciplines. Centers are the natural outgrowth of this middle school model of teaming.

Larger high schools moving toward the small schools concept are creating career academies with an interdisciplinary teaching team. This, too, lends itself easily to becoming a center of pedagogy. In another case, a small elementary school (K–8) has already formed vertical teams across grade levels to foster a learner-centered curriculum. These vertical teams, again, are natural teams for developing centers. Or teachers can informally form their own ad hoc teams using a grassroots approach simply by talking to some other teachers about the concept of the centers of pedagogy. The possibilities are endless. The teams, once formed, would stay together over time, with additions and omissions occurring through natural attrition.

The role of the principal, as alluded to earlier, may be to appoint head teachers for the various teams. The principal may also guide the structure and functions of the centers by providing leadership training on mentoring models. And, in a more practical vein, the principal may facilitate the teams and centers by scheduling time for teams to meet on a regular basis. Often, if some quality time is set aside on the master schedule, the teams will find lots of other time, on their own, to meet and complete the tasks they have set.

There is a sense of community, a sense of spirit, and a sense of collaboration.

In these centers of pedagogy, there is a sense of community, a sense of spirit, and a sense of collaboration. They embody the power of think tanks and the empathy of close-knit families. They have a depth and breadth of human resources that enhance and embellish the work of all on the team. There is an energy and synergy in these spheres of influence that affirm and confirm the members within. They are centers of expertise and encouragement, experience and excitement, empathy and energy.

To better understand these centers of pedagogy, this chapter examines the composition of these three natural spheres of influence: formal mentors (the leaders and sages); practical mentors (career and developing teachers); and collegial mentors (novices and beginning teachers). Although the actual roles within these spheres of influence may not separate as neatly in the real world as they do on paper, they represent the differing influences on the ongoing development of teachers throughout their careers. Box 9.1 shows how these three spheres are defined.

Centers of Pedagogy: The Spheres

Formal mentors/coaches: Leaders and sages

Practical mentors/coaches: Career teachers and developing teachers

Collegial mentors/coaches: Novices and beginning teachers

Box 9.1

Box 9.2 delineates the expected influence of the various spheres. Although these are generalizations of the influences and vary greatly from team to team, the delineation gives some sense of the differences that naturally occur in any community of learners.

Centers of Pedagogy: The Influence

Formal mentors/coaches: Expertise and encouragement

Practical mentors/coaches: Experience and excitement

Collegial mentors/coaches: Empathy and energy

Box 9.2

Formal Mentors

This sphere of influence is comprised of head teachers, professors, and faculty doctoral candidates. They are acknowledged as the leaders and the sages in educational circles. Most likely, they already serve as department heads or team leaders and are recognized voices in the field (present at conferences and perhaps published authors). These formal mentors are valued for their depth of knowledge and their passion and unwavering sense of commitment to the profession as a whole.

Critical to the interactions within the centers of pedagogy, formal mentors take responsibility to share their expertise and encourage others toward excellence. One may be an on-site leader with some teaching responsibilities; the other may be on loan by the university to act as liaison with school staff or a particular faculty team; or another might be part of the faculty working on a doctorate. These professors are solicited as partners and colleagues from nearby universities and colleges.

These formal leaders provide an aura of intellectual discourse.

Together, these formal leaders provide an aura of intellectual discourse to the centers of pedagogy. They provide the inextricable linkages between theory and practice. They ground the center with sound pedagogical understandings that translate into effective classroom practice. These formal mentors keep the lines of communication open between the proverbial ivory tower and the realities of the public school system.

Formal mentors collaboratively plan learning opportunities for their centers and formally introduce and revisit key philosophical issues. They keep the conceptual conversations alive and well as the team strives to learn and excel.

In addition to sharing their expertise, formal mentors keep the spirit alive while encouraging the team to pursue areas of talent and interest. These formal mentors understand the need for all teachers to continue to grow and follow their own passions as they unfold as professionals.

These formal mentors troubleshoot immediate concerns and help the team keep a positive outlook on things. They encourage productive problem solving for ongoing situations and offer encouraging words along the way. The formal mentors have seen it all and soothe and reassure as the pressures of frontline teaching sometimes overwhelm even the most confident teachers.

In summary, the formal mentor role is the mind, body, and spirit of the centers. They set the tone and the expectations for the team. They determine the amount and level of action and interaction. The formal mentors truly are the leaders and sages in this community of learners, as suggested in Box 9.3.

> *The formal mentor role is the mind, body, and spirit of the centers.*

Practical Mentors/Coaches

Practical mentors form the second sphere of influence within the centers of pedagogy. This sphere captures loyal and hard-working career teachers and intermediary or developing teachers ensconced firmly in their teaching careers. These are the models and coaches who thrive in the classroom atmosphere. They know kids, and they know curricular content. These are the proud practitioners who have it all figured out. Observing their classrooms gives the viewer as much implicit information about the inner workings of schooling as do the explicit demonstrations

> *They know kids, and they know curricular content.*

Formal Mentors/Coaches:
Expertise and Encouragement

Expertise: share knowledge about particular grade levels, departments, or disciplines; demonstrate skillful teaching methods; structure curriculum development and inquire about assessment techniques; understand linkages between theory and practice; value school-university collaborations.

Encouragement: provide clarity about goals and objectives; help set priorities; troubleshoot immediate concerns; solve ongoing problem situations; offer encouraging suggestions; model collegial partnerships.

Box 9.3

about instructional methods. In fact, usually these teachers are noticeably passionate about their teaching, and they are continually innovative in their ever amazing classroom practice.

Whether a career teacher or an experienced teacher at the top of the learning curve, these are the mentors who offer the practical, nitty-gritty, nuts-and-bolts kind of advice that bring theories alive. These are the front-line teachers who demonstrate exquisite management techniques from smooth work flow patterns to complex thinking models that get learners intensely involved. These practical mentors have strategies for every situation, from just the right motivation for well-disciplined class behavior at the assembly to magical teaching techniques for those proverbial sticky-wicket kinds of lessons that puzzle kids and teachers alike. These are the mentors who offer, time after time, the teacher-tested, tried-and-true solutions to the unending parade of episodes that plague the less experienced teachers.

The skilled teacher knows just how to reach that reluctant learner and just which entry point to learning will infuse him or her with the confidence to proceed and give it the best shot. These practical mentors are the line coaches who are close to the action and ready to give their protégés insightful feedback that fine-tunes or fixes whatever is going wrong at that moment.

They understand when to talk informally and when a more formal conference is needed with the beginners. They know how to generate excitement in others because it is inbred in their very being. They are teachers, and they love what they do. Their enthusiasm is contagious, and they naturally bring a fever to their work that others cannot help but buy into. With their vast experience and burning passion for kids and for teaching, these practical mentors form the heart and soul of the centers of pedagogy.

As depicted in Box 9.4, these models and coaches provide a spectrum of practical experience to everyday classroom situations. They provide dynamic forums for demonstration teaching, and they keep the excitement in the classroom and in the centers of pedagogy . . . every day, for every student, and for

These practitioners are doing something they love doing, something they cannot imagine not doing.

every teacher on the team. These practitioners are doing something they love doing, something they cannot imagine not doing. It's as simple and as rewarding as that.

Collegial Mentors/Coaches

Collegial mentors comprise a third sphere of influence in the centers of pedagogy envisioned here. They are the novices and beginning faculty members who are somewhat new to the teaching game. They are on a sharp learning curve. It's about survival in the classroom, every day, seven hours a day; every week, five days a week; every month, for nine months a year.

Practical Mentors/Coaches: Experience and Excitement

Experience: demonstrate teaching methods, diverse instructional strategies, flexible teaching/learning strategies, and versatile entry points for learning; give feedback and coaching; structure formal and informal conferences.

Excitement: work closely in classrooms, share stories about students, dissect incidents, capture teachable moments, facilitate day-to-day interactions, give specific feedback, cheer their colleagues on.

Box 9.4

If the formal mentors form the mind, body, and spirit and the practical mentors the heart and soul of the centers, these collegial mentors are the lifeblood.

If the formal mentors form the mind, body, and spirit and the practical mentors the heart and soul of the centers, these collegial mentors are the lifeblood. They bring a continual flow of new blood into the teams. They may be the neediest ones in the team because their needs are immediate and often urgent. But they also may be the most appreciative because they understand the giving of others that's helping them survive. And these fresh, new members of the staff feel genuine empathy for others immersed in similar circumstances.

The collegial mentors are the colleagues and the counselors. They want to listen to others' stories because they want to tell theirs. A professor once said, "If one wants to know what is going on in a school, all one has to do is to listen to the stories teachers tell in the teachers' lunchroom."

"When someone asks me, 'How was your day?' I never know what to answer. I have thirty-one days, every day, a different day with each child." (Codell, 1999).

Stories are the legacies passed on from year to year, teacher to teacher, grade to grade, school to school. Through these stories, teachers share those familiar incidents that make or break a teacher on a particular day. In her outlandish commentary on her first year of teaching, Esme (Codell, 1999) put it this way: "When someone asks me, 'How was your day?' I never know what to answer. I have thirty-one days, every day, a different day with each child" (p. 160).

So, the stories get to the feelings, and the feelings are universal. The feelings, the frustrations, the triumphs of the day are never right or wrong—they just are. When someone is willing to listen and care, then empathy is born. It's so close to home. It rings so true because it's their story, too.

As described in Box 9.5, collegial mentors offer empathy to colleagues and collaborate in counseling each other through some of the tough times.

Collegial Mentors/Coaches

Empathy: listen to real worries, care and understand the weight of the concerns, be "there" when things happen, express sympathy, share, become genuine friends, offer a "safe zone."

Energy: teach peers, dialogue with partners, keep emotions high, develop collaborative efforts, bring experiences and energy to the team, model learning behaviors for each other.

Box 9.5

This sphere of influence must not be underestimated in the centers of pedagogy. These are not just sympathetic ears for the daily gripe session, although there is a need for that kind of safe zone.

Centers of Pedagogy: Spheres of Influence

The dynamics of the centers of pedagogy vary from team to team. The roles played also vary from teacher to teacher. These descriptions are meant to elaborate the concept of the centers, not to limit the possibilities of the composition of the teams or the interaction patterns of those teams. It seems prudent at this point in the discussion, however, to shift the focus to actual structures used in the centers to engage the team in meaningful learning experiences.

Mentoring/coaching experiences seem to fall into five categories as shown in Box 9.6. These include the areas of classroom practice, reflective practice, collaborative planning, new directions, and involvement in the profession itself. For the sake of this discussion, we more fully define the five categories and their purposes and describe the actual learning opportunities within the categories.

Classroom Practice: In the Heat of the Action

Learning opportunities within the microcosm of the classroom are valued highly by effective centers of pedagogy. These are the truly job-embedded kinds of professional development that yield skillful demonstrations and in-depth debriefings (Sparks & Hirsh, 1997). There is probably no other professional development opportunity that can rival this dynamic, authentic, and relevant learning experience. Within the classroom practice category are two models of mentoring that serve different functions. One model of mentoring involves behaviors by the master; the other concerns classroom coaching of a mentee.

Centers of Pedagogy: Spheres of Influence

Classroom practice: In the heat of the action

Reflective practice: Stepping back

Collaborative planning: The power of think tanks

New directions: Looking ahead

The professional: Giving back

Box 9.6

Metacognitive Modeling

In what is called "metacognitive modeling," master teachers not only target and model effective instructional strategies but also accompany that modeling with a running monologue or "meta-monologue." They talk before the lesson about what they are going to do and why they are going

> *They talk before the lesson about what they are going to do and why they are going to do it.*

to do it. During the demonstration, the master teacher may make some pointed editorial comments to highlight specific procedures. And, finally, following the model demonstration, there is a full debriefing about the what, the why, and the how. These demonstrations serve as integral parts of the accepted training model depicted by Joyce and Showers in *Student Achievement Through Staff Development* (1995) and by Moye in *Conditions That Support Transfer for Change* (1997). The elements cited in sound training experiences include theory, demonstration, practice, and coaching. Of course, this fulfills the demonstration portion of the model and helps the protégé better understand what the theory looks and sounds like in the classroom.

Classroom Coaching

The classroom coaching model is the other true job-embedded model of professional development. In this scenario, in a preconference, coach and teacher target the lesson objectives and the planned lesson sequence that the teacher is to perform. Some discussion ensues between them about the expected student reactions and key points to emphasize in the lesson design. Shortly thereafter, the teaching episode occurs with both the teacher and coach in the classroom. Although the teacher takes the lead role, of course, the coach may intervene appropriately during the execution of the lesson if a teachable moment reveals itself. But the substantive debriefing occurs during a postteaching session that follows the actual lesson. In these postconference sessions, reflective questions are in order: What went well? What might you do differently? What help do you need? These are the appropriate cues that spark the meaningful self-analysis that is the focus of the coaching model.

Reflective Practice: Stepping Back

Removed by a step from the actual "in-the-heat-of-the-action" classroom practice are strategies in the reflective practice category that offer opportunities to step back and think about teaching practices. These reflective moments may occur in spontaneous ways or in more formally scheduled times, but the value of these mindful conversations is in this vein called "reflective practice."

Partner Dialogues

Partner dialogues are characterized by two strengths: the one-on-one interaction and the quality time inherent in a partnership. One on one is as good as it gets in terms of attention and involvement in a conversation. The quality of the discussion is high because dialogue tends to track— point by point, point by counterpoint—the exact focus of a topic or idea. Time is well spent, usually in a structured dialogue that targets reflective thinking. This is the purpose and the power of the dialogue format.

Reflections Through Journals

Although person-to-person dialogue fosters reflection through another's voice, reflective journaling harnesses the power of the inner voice. Nothing is quite like the reflective moments that occur as one sits quietly with pen in hand to ponder a real concern. The hand may begin to write quite mundane thoughts and then, suddenly, a moment of clarity, a real insight, an Aha! moment occurs right there on the page. Or after writing, in the rereading perhaps, a connection is made or a next step is revealed. This kind of reflective writing provides the momentary solitude needed to think deeply and internalize the essence of something.

Team Debriefings

Sometimes the most helpful reflection emerges from a teamwide debriefing of an episode or concern. It is the synergy that forms when the group puts its collective mind to an idea. It is a powerfully expansive strategy because of the many diverse perspectives that come into play. Each viewpoint informs the group with another dimension to consider.

Each viewpoint informs the group with another dimension to consider.

As always and by definition, the synergistic energy produces an end product far greater than the mere sum of its parts. These group debriefings are often a regular feature of the centers of pedagogy.

Video Analysis of Lesson

Although some teachers are reluctant to be videotaped during a lesson and participate in an analysis of that lesson, the absolute brilliance of this reflective strategy cannot be overstated. Nothing offers as much authentic feedback as that reflection of oneself from the mirror that the videotaped lesson provides. Of course, the caution is to view the tape with a fair and unbiased state of mind. Often the teacher featured on the tape tends to focus on how she or he looks, tends to become self-critical rather than objectively focus on the techniques used in the teaching. Yet this is a highly valued tool for providing opportunities for personally relevant kinds of reflective practice and feedback (Joyce & Showers, 1995). In fact, the National Board for Professional Teaching Standards (1997) requires two videotaped lessons as part of their professional portfolio process.

Professional Portfolio Process

The reflective practice of developing a professional portfolio (Burke, 1997; Dietz, 1998) involves two equally important elements: the process of developing the portfolio and the portfolio itself as a final product for review. The *process* provides opportunity for goal setting, action research projects in the classroom, problem solving, and demonstration of growth and development, whereas the portfolio as *product* provides the evidence and reflection of the journey. Valuing one over the other defeats the robust reflections afforded by the professional portfolio process because, by virtue of its inherent nature, the reflective process continues over the length of the endeavor. It's a long-term rather than an episodic strategy. The portfolio process is a journey of learning.

Collaborative Planning: The Power of Think Tanks

One of the most frequent activities at the centers of pedagogy is the hands-on planning sessions that are scheduled on a regular basis. These sessions tap into the power of the think tank. These brainstorming sessions lead to piggybacking of ideas, and the results are often more robust than when the planning is done by one teacher insulated from the richness of experiences revealed in a group interaction.

These sessions tap into the power of the think tank.

Curriculum Development

Large poster paper and graphic organizers are the practical tools that foster effective team planning during curricular development sessions. Depicting ideas in a grid or matrix or representing the curriculum as a sequence or listing of ideas that all can see sparks further thinking and associations. The team planner, as these large graphics are called, also provides a viable measure of productivity for team-planning sessions. When the goal of the meeting is to finish the cycle of thinking that completes the graphic planner, the focus is there for uninterrupted work and the accountability factor kicks in. Things get done! It's as simple as that. The planning tool of the graphic becomes a visible, achievable goal to accomplish, and team planning takes on a sense of urgency that is hard to find in the commotion of the teaching day.

Instructional Design

As with curricular planning, instructional design also benefits from a team approach. This provides an opportunity to share winning ideas that work with a particular group or within specific settings. This is a time to bounce ideas off others and to see what bounces back. This is a time for thinking outside the box for innovative and improved instructional results. Again, this is a time to use the large poster board and graphic tools that let the group in on thinking as it is occurring. The team planner is the operative tool for instructional planning sessions as well as for curricular planning sessions. Again, it is the absolute power and synergy of the think tank that makes this a much needed activity of the teams at the center. Naturally, after the team initiates the plan, there are plenty of opportunities for either individuals or pairs of teachers to fine-tune and refine the final design.

Assessment Techniques

To round out planning opportunities, the realm of accountability is always a focal point for the teams at the centers. There are ongoing discussions that take advantage of the strength of collaborative planning about appropriate assessments. These conversations lead to a deeper understanding of the relationship between the curriculum and the standards and ways to prioritize both. They clarify the role of tests in the district and help students and parents know how best to prepare and approach the tests. Assessment is an integral part of the planning process, and the team model lends itself to this endeavor.

New Directions: Looking Ahead

Naturally, much of the activity of the teams at these centers of pedagogy focuses on the impending and immediate needs of the day-to-day demands of the teachers. However, there also is a need to use some of the team time to look at what innovations are on the horizon and what lies ahead in terms of career opportunities. After all, these centers are intended to provide a mentoring model for all teachers throughout the various stages of their career.

Book Studies

The book study is a simple, short-term strategy that can propel a team into thinking about innovation. Members reach consensus about a particular book on the educational scene and plot a course of readings and discussions. This process may involve only four or five sessions in its entirety, yet the impact of exploring a theory with others often has far-reaching consequences for the team's future direction.

Action Research

Another viable tool for the center is the engagement of a member or several members in authentic research in the classroom, that is, action research. Based in real-world situations that occur in K–12 classrooms, teachers have fertile ground for finding rich areas of investigation that yield meaningful results. These personally relevant projects may involve instructional, curricular, or assessment issues or tap into the areas of classroom management, discipline, or even the affective domain of the classroom. Whatever the focus, action research is a profoundly rewarding experience for teachers because of its immediacy to their needs.

> *Whatever the focus, action research is a profoundly rewarding experience for teachers because of its immediacy to their needs.*

Career Counseling

Although career counseling may seem extraneous to the core mission of the mentor program for teachers early in their careers, it is really never too early to begin those lifelong discussions. This can be an extremely rewarding and far-reaching benefit to the team members as the spectrum of career opportunities unfolds. Some may want to begin their master's degree program or pursue certification by the National Board for Professional Teaching Standards. Others may want to consider an administrative path; still others may favor a career path in curriculum or staff development. Whatever their focus, teachers need to begin the conversations early, for it's the stuff that keeps them in the profession.

The Professional: Giving Back

For the teachers who are passionate about the work they do, there is no greater joy than to give something back to the profession. To share a no-fail strategy with a department team, describe a classroom scenario that touches another teacher, or simply explore an idea about the art and science of teaching that needs some percolating time lets the teacher who gives back feel darn good! Sharing is accomplished through writings, essays, articles for professional journals, or presentations at professional gatherings and conferences. Both methods, whether written or oral, have internal rewards for the teachers involved.

Professional Writing

"We write to taste life twice" (Nin, 1992). To have an idea worth sharing is the gift of every skillful teacher. But to actually write the idea, to share it in a formal way, is an entirely different matter. Yet it is the articles written by the practitioners that teachers want to read. It seems that these centers of pedagogy are great training grounds for this kind of noteworthy endeavor. They have the ever fruitful think tank atmosphere, and they have a bank of built-in editors and critics to hone a first draft into a finely tuned finished product.

> "We write to taste life twice"
> (Nin, 1992).

Professional Organizations

Let us offer a final thought about these busy beehives, these centers of pedagogy. The goal is not only to belong to professional organizations but also to take leadership roles of significance and influence. Serving as an officer, presenting at conferences, and taking on temporary tasks are the ways teachers demonstrate their commitment to the profession. These are the ways teachers strive to excel at their chosen work.

The vision presented in this book embodies the philosophical perspectives of contemporary teachers. If they come into the profession, they usually have made an explicit choice to do so. The days of teaching and nursing as the only career options for young women are long gone. The men and the women who enter this profession have given it careful consideration. The people who come to teaching arrive with a caring and a calling. It is up to the educational community to see that their vision is not tarnished in those first fragile years. What better way to foster that vision than to build community and infuse skills and spirit into that community on a regular and ongoing basis.

TOOLS TO USE ■

1. Respond to the Quote

"To teach is to learn."

2. Spheres of Influence

Identify people of influence in your life and people whom you've had the honor of influencing in return.

Someone who influenced me . . .

Someone whom I have influenced . . .

3. Identify . . .

A formal mentor/coach

A practical mentor/coach

A collegial mentor/coach

Take a moment and think back over your professional career and identify those who have honored you with their expertise and their counsel. These may be the very same people listed above as people who have influenced you significantly in some way.

Bibliography

Backer, L., Deck, M., & McCallum, D. (1995). *The presenter's survival kit: It's a jungle out there.* St. Louis, MO: Mosby-Year Book.

Bellanca, J. (1990). *The cooperative think tank: Graphic organizers to teach thinking in the cooperative classroom.* Thousand Oaks, CA: Corwin Press.

Bellanca, J. (1995). *Designing professional development for change.* Thousand Oaks, CA: Corwin Press.

Bellanca, J., & Fogarty, R. (2003). *Blueprints for achievement in the cooperative classroom* (2nd ed.). Thousand Oaks, CA: Corwin Press.

Birnie, W. (1999, Summer). 7 Deadly Sins. *Journal of Staff Development.* Retrieved May 31, 2006, from www2.edc.org/NTP/7deadlysins/7deadlysins.html

Bluestein, J. (Ed.). (1995). *Mentors, masters and Mrs. MacGregor: Stories of teachers making a difference.* Deerfield Beach, FL: Health Communications.

Brennan, S., Tahmes, W., & Roberts, R. (1999). Mentoring with a mission. *Educational Leardership, 56*(8), 49–52.

Burke, K. (1997). *Designing professional portfolios for change.* Thousand Oaks, CA: Corwin Press.

Codell, E. (1999). *Educating Esme: Diary of a teacher's first year.* Chapel Hill, NC: Algonquin Books.

Cordeiro, P., Kraus, C., & Binkowski, K. (1997, March). *A problem-based learning approach to professional development: Supporting learning for transfer.* Paper presented at Annual Meeting of the American Educational Research Association, Chicago, IL.

Cronin, D. (2000). *Click Clack Moo: Cows That Type.* New York: Simon & Schuster.

Cruickshank, D. (1996). *Preparing America's teachers.* Bloomington, IN: Phi Delta Kappa Educational Foundation.

Danielson, C. (1996). *Enhancing professional practice: A framework for teaching.* Alexandria, VA: Association for Supervision and Curriculum Development.

Danielson, C., & McGreal, T. (2000). *Teacher evaluation: To enhance professional practice.* Alexandria, VA: Association for Supervision and Curriculum Development and Princeton, NJ: Educational Testing Service.

Darling-Hammond, L. (1996). *What matters most: A framework for teaching.* Alexandria, VA: Association for Supervision and Curriculum Development.

DeBoer, A. (1986). *The art of consulting.* Chicago: Arcturus Books.

deBono, E. (1973). *Lateral thinking: Creative step by step.* New York: Harper Row.

Denmark, V., & Podsen, I. (2000). The mettle of a mentor. *Journal of Staff Development, 21*(4), 19–22.

Dietz, M. (1998). *Journals as frameworks for change.* Thousand Oaks, CA: Corwin Press.

Fogarty, R. (1991). *How to integrate the curricula.* Thousand Oaks, CA: Corwin Press.

Fogarty, R. (1997). *Brain compatible classrooms.* Thousand Oaks, CA: Corwin Press.

Fogarty, R. (2000). *Ten things new teachers need to succeed.* Thousand Oaks, CA: Corwin Press.

Fogarty, R. (2001a). *Differentiated learning: Different strokes for different folks.* Chicago: Fogarty & Associates.

Fogarty, R. (2001b). *Enhancing transfer.* Chicago: Fogarty & Associates.

Fogarty, R. (2001c). *Finding the time and the money for professional development.* Chicago: Fogarty & Associates.

Fogarty, R. (2001d). *Making sense of the research on the brain and learning.* Chicago: Fogarty & Associates.

Fogarty, R. (2001e). *A mentoring model for our teachers: Centers of pedagogy.* Chicago: Fogarty & Associates.

Fogarty, R. (2001f). Roots of change. *Journal of Staff Development, 21*(3), 34–36.

Fogarty, R. (2001g). *Student learning standards: A blessing in disguise.* Chicago: Fogarty & Associates.

Fogarty, R. (2001h). *Teachers make the difference: A framework of quality.* Chicago: Fogarty & Associates.

Fogarty, R. (2003). *A look at transfer: Seven strategies that work.* Chicago: Fogarty & Associates.

Fogarty, R., & Pete, B. (2003a). *Nine best practices that make the difference.* Chicago: Fogarty & Associates.

Fogarty, R., & Pete, B. (2003b). *Twelve brain principles that make the difference.* Chicago: Fogarty & Associates.

Fogarty, R., & Pete, B. (2004a). *The adult learner: Some things we know.* Chicago: Fogarty & Associates.

Fogarty, R., & Pete, B. (2004b). *A look at transfer: Seven strategies that work.* Chicago: Fogarty & Associates.

Fogarty, R., & Pete, B. (2005a). *Close the achievement gap: Simple strategies that work.* Chicago: Fogarty & Associates.

Fogarty, R., & Pete, B. (2005b). *How to differentiate learning: Curriculum, instruction, assessment.* Chicago: Fogarty & Associates.

Fogarty, R., & Stoehr, J. (1995). *Integrating curriculum with the multiple intelligences: Teams, themes, and threads.* Thousand Oaks, CA: Corwin Press.

Fullan, M. (1982). *The meaning of educational change.* New York: Teachers College Press.

Fullan, M., & Stiegelbauer, E. (1991). *The new meaning of educational change.* New York: Teachers College.

Gardner, H. (1983). *Frames of mind: The theory of multiple intelligences.* New York: Basic Books.

Garmston, R., & Wellman, B. (1992). *How to make presentations that teach and transfer.* Alexandria, VA: Association for Curriculum and Development.

Garvin, D. A. (2000). *Learning into action: A guide to putting the learning organization to work.* Cambridge, MA: Harvard Business School Press.

Gladwell, M. (2000). *The tipping point.* Boston: Little, Brown.

Goodlad, J. (1983). *A place called school: Prospects for the future.* New York: McGraw-Hill.

Gordon, S. (1991). *How to help beginning teachers succeed.* Alexandria, VA: Association for Supervision and Curriculum Development.

Gousie, G. (1997, May). *Speaking with confidence.* Paper presented at the National Head Start Association, Boston, MA.

Grant, J., & Forsten, C. (1999). *If you're riding a horse and it dies, get off.* Peterborough, NH: Crystal Springs Books.

Guskey, T. (2000). *Evaluating professional development.* Thousands Oaks, CA: Corwin Press.

Halford, J. (1998). Easing the way for new teachers. *Educational Leadership, 55*(5), 33–36.

Hall, G., & Hord, S. (1987*). Change in schools, facilitating the process.* Albany: State University of New York.

Hargreaves, A. (1994). *Changing teachers, changing times: Teacher's work and culture in the post modern age.* New York: Teachers College Press.

Hoffman, R. (1998). *I can see you naked: A fearless guide to making great presentations.* New York: Andrews & McMeel.

Hughes, P. (Ed.). (1991). *Teachers in society: Teachers' professional development.* Victoria: Australian Council for Educational Research.

Johnson, D. W., Johnson, R. T., & Holubec, E. J. (1986). *Circles of learning: Cooperation in the classroom.* Alexandria, VA: Association for Supervision and Curriculum Development.

Johnson, D. W., Johnson, R. T., & Holubec, E. J. (1998). *Cooperation in the classroom.* Edina, MN: Interaction Book.

Johnson, S. (1998). *Who moved my cheese?* New York: Putnam's Sons.

Johnson, S. (1998). *Who moved my cheese?* [Audiotape]. New York: Simon & Schuster.

Joyce, B., & Showers, B. (1983). *Power in staff development through research on training.* Alexandria, VA: Association for Supervision and Curriculum Development.

Joyce, B., & Showers, B. (1995). *Student achievement through staff development.* New York: Longman.

Joyce, B., & Showers, B. (2002). *Student achievement through staff development.* Alexandria, VA: Association for Supervision and Curriculum Development.

Kagan, S. (1989.) Cooperation works. *Educational Leadership. 47*(4), 12–15.

Killion, J. (1999, Winter). Knowing when and how much to steer the ship. *Journal of Staff Development,* 59–60.

Knowles, M. (1973). *The adult learner: A neglected species.* Houston, TX: Gulf Professional.

Knowles, M., Holton, E., & Swanson, R. (1998). *The adult learner: The definitive classic in adult education and human resource development* (5th ed.). Woburn, MA: Butterworth-Heinemann.

Krupp, J. (1981). *Adult development: Implications for staff development.* Manchester, CT: Judy Erin Krupp.

Krupp, J. (1982). *The adult learner: A unique entity.* Manchester, CT: Judy Erin Krupp.

Lieberman, A. (Ed.). (1988). *Building a professional culture in schools.* New York: Teachers College Press.

Lieberman, A., & Miller, L. (2000). Teaching and teacher development: A synthesis for a new century. In R. S. Brandt (Ed.), *Education in a new era.* Alexandria, VA: Association for Supervision and Curriculum Development.

Little, J. W. (1975). The power of organizational setting: School norms and staff development. Paper adapted from final report to National Institute on Education, *School success and staff development: The role of staff development in urban desegregated schools,* 1981.

Moye, V. (1997). *Conditions that support transfer for change.* Thousand Oaks, CA: Corwin Press.

National Board for Professional Teaching Standards. (1997). *What teachers should know and be able to do.* Washington, DC: Author.

Nin, A. (1992). *Quote on Seabright Press/Contemporary Artists* [greeting card]. Santa Cruz, CA: Seabright.

Parnes, S. (1975). *Aha insights into creative behavior.* Buffalo, NY: DOK.

Perkins, D., & Solomon, G. (1987). *Teaching for transfer in developing minds: A resource book for teaching thinking* (3rd ed.). Alexandria, VA: Association for Supervision and Curriculum Development.

Pete, B., & Sambo, C. (2004) *Data! Dialogue! Decisions! The data difference.* Chicago, IL: Fogarty & Associates.

Pike, R., & Arch, D. (1997). *Dealing with difficult participants.* San Francisco: Jossey-Bass.

Pitton, D. (2000). *Mentoring novice teachers: Fostering a dialogue process.* Thousand Oaks, CA: Corwin Press.

Purnell, S., & Hill, P. (1992). *Time for reform.* Santa Monica, CA: RAND.

Radin, J. (1998, February). So, you want to be an educational consultant? *The School Administrator.* Retrieved June 2, 2006, from http://www.aasa.org/publications

Robbins, P. (1999). Mentoring. *Journal of Staff Development, 20*(3), 40–42.

Rowley, J., & Hart, P. (1999). *Mentoring the new teacher* [videocassettes]. Alexandria, VA: Association for Supervision and Curriculum Development.

Sarasan, S. (1982). *The culture of school and the problem of change* (2nd ed.). Boston: Allyn & Bacon.

Scearce, C. (1992). *100 ways to build teams.* Thousand Oaks, CA: Corwin Press.

Schmoker, M. (1996) *Results: The key to continuous school improvement.* Alexandria, VA: Association of Supervision and Curriculum Development.

Schmuck, R. (1997). *Practical action research for change.* Thousand Oaks, CA: Corwin Press.

Schmuck, R., & Schmuck, P. (1997). *Group processes in the classroom.* Madison, WI: Brown and Benchmark.

Sparks, D., & Hirsh, S. (1997). *A new vision for staff development.* Alexandria, VA: Association for Supervision and Curriculum Development.

Sparks, D., & Loucks-Horsley, S. (1990). *Five models of staff development.* Oxford, OH: National Staff Development Council.

Stern, N., & Payment, M. (1995). *101 stupid things trainers do to sabotage success.* Irvine, CA: Richard Chang Associates.

Sweeny, B. (2001). *Leading the teacher induction and mentoring program.* Thousand Oaks, CA: Corwin Press.

Tate, M. (2004). *Lessons learned: 20 instructional strategies that engage the adult mind.* Thousands Oaks, CA: Corwin Press.

Van Ekeren, G. (1994). *Speaker's sourcebook II: Quotes, stories and anecdotes for every occasion.* Paramus, NJ: Prentice Hall.

Wang, N., & Taraban, R. (1997). *Do learning strategies affect adults' transfer of learning?* (ERIC Document Reproduction Service No. ED413 419)

Whitaker, S. (2000). Informal, available, patient. *Journal of Staff Development, 21*(4), 23.

Williams, R. B. (1996, Winter). Four dimensions of the school change facilitator. *Journal of Staff Development,* 48–50.

William, R. B. (1996). *More than 50 ways to build team consensus* [Training Package]. Thousand Oaks, CA: Corwin Press.

Williams, R. B. (1997). *Twelve roles of the facilitator for school change.* Thousand Oaks, CA: Corwin Press.

Wohlsletter, P. (1997). *Organizing for successful school-based management.* Alexandria, VA: Association of Supervision and Curriculum Development.

Wong, H., & Wong, R. (1998). *How to be an effective teacher: The first days of school.* Mountain View, CA: Harry Wong.

Zemke, R., & Zemke, S. (1981, June). 30 things we know for sure about adult learning. *Training, the Magazine of Human Development,* 45–52.

Index